happiness
a-z

The Gleeful Guide to Finding and Following Your Bliss

by Louise Baxter Harmon
Foreword by June Cotner

D0594716

Published in the United States by Viva Editions, an imprint of Start Midnight, LLC, 609 Greenwich Street, Sixth Floor, New York, New York, 10014.

Printed in the United States.
Cover design: Scott Idleman/Blink
Cover photograph: iStockphoto
Text design: Frank Wiedemann

First Edition.
10 9 8 7 6 5 4 3 2 1

Print book ISBN: 978-1-63228-007-7
E-book ISBN: 978-1-63228-0113-8

Library of Congress Cataloging-in-Publication Data

Harmon, Louise.
 Happiness A to Z : the gleeful guide to finding and following your bliss / Louise Baxter Harmon. -- First edition.
    pages cm
 Includes bibliographical references and index.
 ISBN 978-1-63228-007-7 (paperback)
1. Self-actualization (Psychology)--Quotations, maxims, etc. 2. Motiva-tion (Psychology)--Quotations, maxims, etc. I. Title.
 BF637.S4H346 2015
 158--dc23
                    2014042194

Contents

Foreword

by June Cotner

HAPPINESS A TO Z offers refreshing perspectives on happiness from a wide variety of experts, including classic writers Albert Camus, Emily Dickinson, and Kahlil Gibran, as well as contemporary figures such as Drew Barrymore, Deepak Chopra, and Oprah Winfrey.

Having spent the last twenty years compiling inspirational collections, I was delighted to find this easy-to-use happiness guide! I'm committed to the power of inspirational thoughts and believe they can dramatically improve our lives. A positive perspective is the foundation of happiness—and *Happiness A to Z* will provide you with hundreds of inspiring quotes!

The book is conveniently divided into A-Z chapters such as "Bliss," "Kindness," "Purpose," and "Wonder." Author Louise Baxter Harmon introduces each chapter with personal reflections and ideas you can apply to your own life. Many of her reflections deal with the "inner workings" of happiness and, with each reading, these uplifting thoughts will affect your life in ever more positive ways.

Open the book to any page and let more happiness come into your life today!

June Cotner

Author of *Garden Blessings* and *Graces*

Introduction

What I Know for Sure about Happiness

WOULDN'T IT BE nice if happiness could be guaranteed just by learning your ABCs? While this inspired idea would seemingly make it as easy as following a recipe, experiencing happiness is not quite that simple. As it turns out, though, there is a language for this most-desired state of being, a vocabulary describing the art of contentment. From becoming a vessel to be filled with joy, to allowing yourself to be a little silly now and then, to becoming one with bliss, there are many words and many ways to be happy.

Happiness, as the old adage goes, is definitely an inside job. The inner work of happiness is that of thinking about how you live your life and how your thinking is foundational. We all know that where we were born, to whom we were born and the circumstances greatly influence who we are at the beginning of our lives, but this is not the alpha and the omega of who we are. By applying yourself at school, at work, in life, doors can open in any circumstance. Who you are is who you think you are. If you believe you are a person with potential, your potential will unfold. Many of us receive what I call negative programming when we are young and impressionable, but this can't become the determining factor. Erase those old tapes and write your own program! Easier said than done, I know, but self-belief is the key. If it means writing affirmations and putting them on the fridge at home, then do it. If it means working with a life coach, try it. Perhaps consider an analytical approach, or process mapping your life and seeing how you come to be at a place in your life where you need to unlearn some old, bad unhappiness habits. Maybe for you, it would entail a retreat at Esalen learning yoga and deepest meditation. Or it could be simple, doable steps like getting up earlier in the day and trying one new thing a day.

The happiness pointers in this book are various approaches to inner work, ranging from a more spiritual path to simple and practical everyday tasks. Not every single one of these suggestions will work for you, but some of them will, so sift through the wisdom shared here by generous happiness practitioners and see what strikes a chord within you. What kind of happiness are you seeking? Maybe you don't know yet—or you thought you did, but now you are not so sure. Maybe you are on the right track but just need a gentle nudge in a new direction. In our own lives, happiness can feel transitory and elusive. We can get overwhelmed by business and commit the cardinal "happiness eradicator" of comparing ourselves to others. Thinking about what you lack is the shortest path to misery that I know of. Instead, do a reframe and think about what you have; gifts, talents, positive people in your life, a great garden, all the great, good things in your life. Better already, right? You'll feel even better once you have read these surefire ways to get happy. Many great philosophers thought long and hard about the topic of human happiness and I find that, as I grow older, I agree more with the great Erasmus who was figuring it all about 500 years ago:

> *The summit of happiness is reached when a person is ready to be what he is.*

Louise Baxter Harmon

Alive

Savor Each Moment
All of Your Days

WHETHER THIS WORLD began as the biblical story of Genesis tells us, or as a happy accident post-"Big Bang," it is nothing less than a miracle that we are *alive* and get to share this experience with the people (and animals!) we love. The advice from the wise women and men gathered in this book is to "live it up!" Guzzle every delicious drop of joy and just really go for it! So, ramp it up and amp it up, and I advise you to fully realize what it means to be completely alive. From being truly self-aware and embracing your health and vitality, to maximizing each moment of every day, we encourage you to savor what a it is to be alive in this beautiful world, surrounded by friends, family and loved ones. In the words of the one and only Iggy Pop, "I got a lust for life, oh, yeah!"

Dancing is the loftiest, the most moving, the most beautiful of the arts, because it is no mere translation or abstraction from life; it is life itself.

—HAVELOCK ELLIS

That it will never come again is what makes life so sweet.

—EMILY DICKINSON

We can only be said to be alive in those moments when our hearts are conscious of our treasures.

—THORNTON WILDER

There is a fountain of youth; it is your mind, your talents, the creativity you bring to your life and the lives of the people you love. When you learn to tap this source, you will have truly defeated age.

—SOPHIA LOREN

Life is too tragic for sadness. Let us rejoice.

—EDWARD ABBEY

All I can say about life is, oh God, enjoy it!

—BOB NEWHART

a

Be glad of life because it gives you the chance to love, and to work, and to play, and to look up at the stars.

—HENRY VAN DYKE

One should sympathize with joy, the beauty, the color of life—the less said about life's sores the better.

—OSCAR WILDE

We act as though comfort and luxury were the chief requirements of life, when all that we need to make us really happy is something to be enthusiastic about.

—CHARLES KINGSLEY

I finally figured out the only reason to be alive is to enjoy it.

—RITA MAE BROWN

My point is, life is about balance. The good and the bad. The highs and the lows. The piña and the colada.

—ELLEN DEGENERES

The supreme accomplishment is to blur the line between work and play.

—ARNOLD TOYNBEE

There are to things to aim at in life! First, to get what you want and, after that, to enjoy it. Only the wisest of mankind achieve the second.

—LOGAN PEARSALL SMITH

Exhilaration of life can be found only with an upward look. This is an exciting world. It is cram-packed with opportunity. Great moments wait around every corner.

—RICHARD DEVOS

Life is a pure flame, and we live by an invisible sun within us.

—SIR THOMAS BROWNE

Tomorrow's fate, though thou be wise, thou canst not tell nor yet surmise; pass, therefore, not today in vain, for it will never come again.

—OMAR KHAYYÁM

a

It matters not how long we live, but how.

—PHILIP JAMES BAILEY

Here is the test to find whether your mission on Earth is finished: if you're alive, it isn't.

—RICHARD BACH

Sooner or later that which is now life shall be poetry, and every fair and manly trait shall add a richer strain to the song.

—RALPH WALDO EMERSON

I finally know the difference between pleasing and loving, obeying and respecting. It has taken me so many years to be okay with being different, and with being this alive, this intense.

—EVE ENSLER

I've lived and loved.

—FRIEDRICH SCHILLER

My life is like the summer rose, That opens to the morning sky, But, ere the shades of evening close, Is scattered on the ground—to die!

—R. H. WILDE

Not knowing when the dawn will come, I open every door.

—EMILY DICKINSON

The whole point of being alive is to evolve into the complete person you were intended to be.

—OPRAH WINFREY

Life is short. If you doubt me, ask a butterfly. Their average lifespan is a mere five to fourteen days.

—ELLEN DEGENERES

alive

Bliss

The Highest Level of Consciousness

THE GREAT MYTHOGRAPHER Joseph Campbell famously said, "Follow your bliss," and thus instilled this idea into millions of minds and hearts. Campbell quite generously gave us all permission to seek out our true destiny, even inspiring Campbell fanboy George Lucas to center his epic Star Wars series around such concepts, with heroic journeys in service of finding personal destiny. The concept of *bliss* itself is one of the many levels of human happiness. As for me, I believe Joseph Campbell was talking about a higher level of consciousness when he spoke of bliss. Upon reading another of the greats, Huston

Smith, I discovered there are Sanskrit words describing levels above bliss— ecstatic states of being like *sachchidanand* for which there are no English words. Let's add those to our happiness alphabet, shall we? One thing the world's wisdom traditions all agree on is that states of higher being are not attained by stumbling along an unmarked road to blisstown, but are a result of doing inner work and self development. To me, bliss means connecting with your true self more deeply and arriving at a place of ease and awareness.

> *If you do follow your bliss you put yourself on a kind of track that has been there all the while, waiting for you, and the life that you ought to be living is the one you are living. Follow your bliss and don't be afraid, and doors will open where you didn't know they were going to be.*
>
> —JOSEPH CAMPBELL

Fragrance can have a great effect on our well-being, triggering happy memories or unlocking our sensuality. Indulge in some new oils, candles, or perfumes and enjoy the results.

—NANCY KLINE

Nothing is more important than reconnecting with your bliss. Nothing is as rich. Nothing is more real.

—DEEPAK CHOPRA

Alone let him constantly meditate in solitude on that which is salutary for his soul, for he who meditates in solitude attains supreme bliss.

—GURU NANAK

It takes patience to appreciate domestic bliss; volatile spirits prefer unhappiness.

—GEORGE SANTAYANA

Where ignorance is bliss, 'tis folly to be wise.

—THOMAS GRAY

Meditation is painful in the beginning but it bestows immortal bliss and supreme joy in the end.

—SWAMI SIVANANDA

Live with integrity, respect the rights of other people, and follow your own bliss.

—NATHANIEL BRANDEN

Materialism is the only form of distraction from true bliss.

—DOUGLAS HORTON

Life is a pilgrimage. The wise man does not rest by the roadside inns. He marches direct to the illimitable domain of eternal bliss, his ultimate destination.

—SWAMI SIVANANDA

The weak have remedies, the wise have joys; superior wisdom is superior bliss.

—EDWARD YOUNG

Life without deadlines is bliss.

—CHRIS DECKER

Some place the bliss in action, some in ease,
those call it pleasure, and contentment
these.

—ALEXANDER POPE

bliss

Only internal bliss is perpetual, nothing else
is created to last. That's why God lives within
us and all storms pass.

—CARL HENEGAN

Our true nature is bliss. That bliss is like
the sun that always shines. It remains ever
present, but the events in life and clouds of
worry, and even emotions like happiness,
may obscure it like storm clouds obscure
the sun.

—DEBRA MOFFITT

BIBLIOBLISS: Transported into states of
transcendent pleasure while immersed in
reading a favorite book.

—ROB BREZSNY

For oft, when on my couch I lie in vacant or in pensive mood, they flash upon that inward eye which is the bliss of solitude; and then my heart with pleasure fills, and dances with the daffodils.

—WILLIAM WORDSWORTH

It's good to be just plain happy. It's a little better to know that you're happy, but to understand that you're happy and to know why and how and still be happy. Be happy in the being and the knowing, well that is beyond happiness, that is bliss.

—HENRY MILLER

To be happy—one must find one's bliss.

—GLORIA VANDERBILT

Condition, circumstance, is not the thing; bliss is the same in subject or king.

—ALEXANDER POPE

Now a soft kiss—Aye, by that kiss, I vow an endless bliss.

—JOHN KEATS

To be overcome by the fragrance of flowers is a delectable form of defeat.

—BEVERLY NICHOLS

Life itself is the proper binge.

—JULIA CHILD

Music melts all the separate parts of our bodies together.

—ANAÏS NIN

No entertainment is so cheap as reading, nor any pleasure so lasting.

—MARY WORTLEY MONTAGU

This very moment is a seed from which the flowers of tomorrow's happiness grow.

—JUSTINE THOREAU

Contentment

Take Your Happiness with You

I HAVE A FRIEND who is an adventure travel guide and writer named Brad Olsen. My nickname for him is "world stomper" because he is six-feet, nine-inches tall and he strides across the globe spreading cheer, exploring beautiful and amazing places, writing and creating art from his journeys. When Brad traveled the Indian subcontinent, he went from the uppermost territories including the Himalayan foothills all the way to the shores of Goa and the spice-filled tropics of Kerala. As I previously mentioned, he is an adventurer, so he visited temples, sacred sites and generally soaked up the myriad cultures

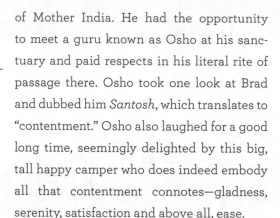 of Mother India. He had the opportunity to meet a guru known as Osho at his sanctuary and paid respects in his literal rite of passage there. Osho took one look at Brad and dubbed him *Santosh*, which translates to "contentment." Osho also laughed for a good long time, seemingly delighted by this big, tall happy camper who does indeed embody all that contentment connotes—gladness, serenity, satisfaction and above all, ease.

I take this story as a good reminder to take your happiness with you wherever you may be. It is the best of ambassadors.

The art of being happy lies in the power of extracting happiness from common things.

—HENRY WARD BEECHER

Money doesn't always bring happiness. People with ten million dollars are no happier than people with nine million dollars.

—HOBART BROWN

I didn't want to be rich. I just wanted enough to get the couch reupholstered.

—KATE (MRS. ZERO) MOSTEL

Measure wealth not by the things you have, but by the things you have for which you would not take money.

—ANONYMOUS

The man is the richest whose pleasures are the cheapest.

—HENRY DAVID THOREAU

A happy woman is one who has no cares at all; a cheerful woman is one who has cares but doesn't let them get her down.

—BEVERLY SILLS

contentment

The happiest and most contented people are those who each day perform to make the best of their abilities.

—ALFRED A. MONTAPERT

The secret of happiness is not in doing what one likes, but in liking what one does.

—J. M. BARRIE

The secret of happiness is to count your blessings while others are adding up their troubles.

—WILLIAM PENN

To be without some of the things you want is an indispensable part of happiness.

—BERTRAND RUSSELL

It is not how much we have, but how much we enjoy, that makes happiness.

—CHARLES SPURGEON

Where wealth and freedom reign, content-ment fails, and honour sinks where commerce long prevail.

—OLIVER GOLDSMITH

Since every man who lives is born to die, and none can boast sincere felicity, with equal mind, what happens let us bear, nor joy nor grieve too much for things beyond our care. Like pilgrims, to th' appointed place we tend; the world's an inn, and death the journey's end.

—JOHN DRYDEN

Joy of life seems to me to arise from a sense of being where one belongs...of being four-square with the life we have chosen. All the discontented people I know are trying sedulously to be something they are not, to do something they cannot do.

—DAVID GRAYSON

At the end of our time on earth, if we have lived fully, we will not be able to say, "I was always happy." Hopefully, we will be able to say, "I have experienced a lifetime of real moments, and many of them were happy moments."

—BARBARA DE ANGELIS

Embracing and appreciating "now" reminds you of what it took to get here.

—DAVID MEZZAPELLE

contentment

Contentment furnishes constant joy. Much covetousness, constant grief. To the contented, even poverty is joy. To the discontented, even wealth is a vexation.

—MING SUM PAOU KEËN

In Paris a queer little man you may see, a little man all in gray; rosy and round as an apple is he, content with the present whate'er it may be, while from care and from cash he is equally free, and merry both night and day! "Ma foi! I laugh at the world," says he, "I laugh at the world and the world laughs at me!" What a gay little man in gray.

—PIERRE-JEAN DE BÉRANGER

Some things are of that nature as to make one's fancy chuckle, while his heart doth ache.

—JOHN BUNYAN

We'll therefore relish with content whate'er kind Providence has sent nor aim beyond our pow'r; for, if our stock be very small, 'tis prudent to enjoy it all, nor lose the present hour.

—NATHANIEL COTTON

Be thankful for what you have; you'll end up having more. If you concentrate on what you don't have, you will never, ever have enough.

—OPRAH WINFREY

It's not getting what you want, it's wanting what you've got.

—SHERYL CROW

Remember, it is one thing to desire success from achievement. It's another to allow money and materialism to blur your view of reality.

—DAVID MEZZAPELLE

Happy the man, of mortals happiest he, whose quiet mind from vain desires is free; whom neither hopes deceive, nor fears torment, but lives at peace, within himself content; in thought, or act, accountable to none but to himself and to the gods alone.

—GEORGE GRANVILLE

How we spend our days is, of course, how we spend our lives.

—ANNIE DILLARD

Delight

A Sudden State of Glee

YOU CAN'T PLAN to be delighted. In fact, it would negate and utterly defeat the purpose. I feel sure that delight has to sneak up and tap you on the shoulder and then alight on that very shoulder. Delight is like a muse: it can be invited, hoped for and received with, well, delight! Delight has effervescence—a sudden state of glee, to be gladdened and oh—so pleased. I would even go so far as to say that delight cannot be suppressed and is best shared as quickly as possible.

So, go forth and have a simply delightful time of it.

If you always do what interests you, at least one person is pleased.

—KATHARINE HEPBURN

People rarely succeed unless they have fun in what they are doing.

—DALE CARNEGIE

Love is like a beautiful flower which I may not touch, but whose fragrance makes the garden a place of delight just the same.

—HELEN KELLER

When you are joyous, look deep into your heart and you shall find it is only that which has given you joy. When you are sorrowful look again in your heart, and you shall see that in truth you are weeping for that which has been your delight.

—KAHLIL GIBRAN

The moment you have in your heart this extraordinary thing called love and feel the depth, the delight, the ecstasy of it, you will discover that for you the world is transformed.

—JIDDU KRISHNAMURTI

A poem begins in delight and ends in wisdom.

—ROBERT FROST

We find delight in the beauty and happiness of children that makes the heart too big for the body.

—RALPH WALDO EMERSON

Birds sing after a storm; why shouldn't people feel as free to delight in whatever remains to them?

—ROSE KENNEDY

Loss is nothing else but change, and change is Nature's delight.

—MARCUS AURELIUS

Silence is the element in which great things fashion themselves together; that at length they may emerge, full-formed and majestic, into the delight of life, which they are thenceforth to rule.

—THOMAS CARLYLE

The soul of sweet delight can never be defiled.

—WILLIAM BLAKE

The true delight is in the finding out rather than in the knowing.

—ISAAC ASIMOV

Only when your consciousness is totally focused on the moment you are in can you receive whatever gift, lesson, or delight that moment has to offer.

—BARBARA DE ANGELIS

It's a delight to trust someone so completely.

—JEFF GOLDBLUM

There is no greater delight than to be conscious of sincerity on self-examination.

—MENCIUS

Not by appointment do we meet delight or joy; They heed not our expectancy; But round some corner of the streets of life they of a sudden greet us with a smile.

—GERALD MASSEY

Imagination, the supreme delight of the immortal and the immature, should be limited. In order to enjoy life, we should not enjoy it too much.

—VLADIMIR NABOKOV

True education flowers at the point when delight falls in love with responsibility.

—PHILIP PULLMAN

There is delight in singing, though none hear besides the singer.

—WALTER SAVAGE LANDOR

You will find truth more quickly through delight than gravity. Let out a little more string on your kite.

—ALAN COHEN

A bird does not sing because he has an answer, he sings because he has a song.

—JOAN WALSH

The more you praise and celebrate your life, the more there is in life to celebrate.

—OPRAH WINFREY

delight

Go for a walk in the rain.

—CYNTHIA MACGREGOR

Take care of the luxuries and the necessities will take care of themselves.

—DOROTHY PARKER

We owe something to extravagance, for thrift and adventure seldom go hand in hand.

—JENNIE JEROME CHURCHILL

Enlightened

A Lifelong Pursuit

AS THE STORY GOES, a young man sat beneath a bodhi tree in old India and became enlightened. Could it really be that simple? Can this state of higher consciousness really be achieved in an instant? As for myself, I will probably never even come close to becoming enlightened, but it does seem to have happened to at least one person when young Siddhartha became Buddha.

For the rest of us, attaining enlightenment will be a lifetime's pursuit and a matter of much inner work, soul searching and serious study of the world's wisdom traditions. Speaking of wise words and great truths, Buddha or any enlightened being would never admit to it, according to the Buddhist teachings. To do so would be to admit you are separate from the rest of humanity and separate from the stream. One of the great masters of spiritual scholarship, Huston Smith has this to say about the subject:

> *Suffering led the Buddha to enlightenment, and it may cause us, against our will, to grow in compassion, awareness, and possibly eventually peace.*

Down deep we really know our worth, but we don't have easy access to that knowledge. We need to hear praise coming from outside ourselves or we don't remember that we deserve it.

—BARBARA SHER

One laugh of a child will make the holiest day more sacred still.

—ROBERT G. INGERSOLL

Happiness is the spiritual experience of living every minute with love, grace, and gratitude.

—DENIS WAITLEY

It is the happiness that comes from within that is lasting and fulfilling.

—LEDDY SCHMELIGH

Blessings star forth forever; but a curse is like a cloud, it passes.

—PHILIP JAMES BAILEY

Merciful Father, I will not complain. I know that the sunshine shall follow the rain.

—JOAQUIN MILLER

enlightened

To enjoy good health, to bring true happiness to one's family, to bring peace to all, one must first discipline and control one's own mind. If a man can control his mind he can find the way to enlightenment, and all wisdom and virtue will naturally come to him.

—SIDDHARTHA GAUTAMA BUDDHA

Knowing others is wisdom, knowing yourself is enlightenment.

—LAO TZU

Enlightenment is the key to everything, and it is the key to intimacy, because it is the goal of true authenticity.

—MARIANNE WILLIAMSON

I would say any behavior that is not the status quo is interpreted as insanity, when, in fact, it might actually be enlightenment. Insanity is sorta in the eye of the beholder.

—CHUCK PALAHNIUK

Ignorance has always been the weapon of tyrants; enlightenment the salvation of the free.

—BILL RICHARDSON

Everyone has a spirit that can be refined, a body that can be trained in some manner, a suitable path to follow. You are here to realize your inner divinity and manifest your innate enlightenment.

—MORIHEI UESHIBA

Always keep your mind as bright and clear as the vast sky, the great ocean, and the highest peak, empty of all thoughts. Always keep your body filled with light and heat. Fill yourself with the power of wisdom and enlightenment.

—MORIHEI UESHIBA

Working with plants, trees, fences and walls, if they practice sincerely they will attain enlightenment.

—DOGEN ZENJI

It isn't by getting out of the world that we become enlightened, but by getting into the world...by getting so tuned in that we can ride the waves of our existence and never get tossed because we become the waves.

—KEN KESEY

Earth and sky, woods and fields, lakes and rivers, the mountain and the sea, are excellent schoolmasters, and teach some of us more than we can ever learn from books.

—JOHN LUBBOCK

Enlightenment is man's leaving his self-caused immaturity.

—IMMANUEL KANT

The true value of a human being can be found in the degree to which he has attained liberation from the self.

—ALBERT EINSTEIN

The road to enlightenment is long and difficult, and you should try not to forget snacks and magazines.

—ANNE LAMOTT

Within each of us is a light, awake, encoded in the fibers of our existence. Divine ecstasy is the totality of this marvelous creation experienced in the hearts of humanity.

—TONY SAMARA

Spirituality is a practical approach to living that can be accessed and strengthened through deliberate attention and the focus that comes from a daily practice.

—POLLY CAMPBELL

Desire, ask, believe, receive.

—STELLA TERRILL MANN

It isn't until you come to a spiritual understanding of who you are—not necessarily a religious feeling, but deep down, the spirit within—that you can begin to take control.

—OPRAH WINFREY

For every way that we can be "mindless" about something, there is a contrasting way to be *mindful*—to approach everything in our lives as a spiritual practice.

—MAGGIE OMAN SHANNON

A woman who is willing to be herself and pursue her own potential runs not so much the risk of loneliness as the challenge of exposure to more interesting men—and people in general.

—LORRAINE HANSBERRY

enlightened

Friendship

Your Friends Are the
Stories You Share

ONE OF MY favorite statements ever made on the subject
is this: "Friendship is not a big thing, it is a million little
things." This is so true. Friends are a constant; you know
your pals can be counted on in a pinch and during emer-
gencies great and small. You also know your true blues will
remember your birthday along with the day your divorce
was final and show up at your door with hugs and a chilled
bottle of exactly the right thing.

But most of all, your friends are the stories you share.

I am lucky to count BJ Gallagher as a friend, and she
wrote an excellent book on this very topic, *Friends Are*

Everything. She covers every aspect of this special kind of love and "adopted family." I love that BJ Gallagher really spells out the nature of true friends with the phrase, "They help us see ourselves more clearly." I'll close with what might be my favorite ever quote on friendship and one I can attest to personally:

> *It's the friends you can call up at 4 a.m. that matter.*
> —MARLENE DIETRICH

True friendship is seen through the heart, not through the eyes.

—ANONYMOUS

Laughter is not at all a bad beginning for a friendship, and it is by far the best ending for one.

—OSCAR WILDE

Life's truest happiness is found in friendships we make along the way.

—ANONYMOUS

The happiest business in all the world is that of making friends, and no investment on the street pays larger dividends, for life is more than stocks and bonds, and love than rate percent, and he who gives in friendship's name shall reap what he has spent.

—ANONYMOUS

The richest man in the world is not the one who still has the first dollar he ever earned. It's the man who still has his best friend.

—MARTHA MASON

If you want an accounting of your worth, count your friends.

—MERRY BROWNE

What a great blessing is a friend with a heart so trusty you may safely bury all your secrets in it.

—SENECA

Of all the things which wisdom provides to make us entirely happy, much the greatest is the possession of friendship.

—EPICURUS

A friend might well be reckoned the masterpiece of nature.

—RALPH WALDO EMERSON

Friendship is the only cement that will ever hold the world together.

—WOODROW WILSON

A real friend is the one who walks in when the rest of the world walks out.

—WALTER WINCHELL

The most I can do for my friend is simply to be his friend.

—HENRY DAVID THOREAU

Friendship improves happiness and abates misery by doubling our joy and dividing our grief.

—JOSEPH ADDISON

It is not what you give your friend, but what you are willing to give him, that determines the quality of your friendship.

—MARY DIXON THAYER

A friend is someone who knows all about you and loves you just the same.

—ELBERT HUBBARD

It is not the talking that counts between friends, it is the never needing to say what counts.

—SHAWN GREEN

True friendship comes when silence between two people is comfortable.

—DAVE TYSON GENTRY

friendship

f

Friendship is a single soul dwelling in two bodies.

—ARISTOTLE

Treat your friends as you do your pictures, and place them in their best light.

—JENNIE JEROME CHURCHILL

Friends will not only live in harmony, but in melody.

—HENRY DAVID THOREAU

Lots of people want to ride with you in the limo, but what you want is someone who will take the bus with you when the limo breaks down.

—OPRAH WINFREY

The best relationships develop out of friendships.

—DIANE KEATON

I can trust my friends. These people force me to examine, encourage me to grow.

—CHER

In a friend you find a second self.

—ISABELLE NORTON

I always felt that the great high privilege, relief, and comfort of friendship was that one had to explain nothing.

—KATHERINE MANSFIELD

friendship

Gratitude

Beauty at Every Turn of the Road

THERE IS AN expression that says if you want to turn your life around, try thankfulness, because finding reasons to be grateful every day can be the key to living an abundant life.

We all know people who find beauty at every turn of the road. They are really and truly grateful for each and every counter—the smile on a stranger's face, the kindness of the grocery store clerk. When you are around these people it sets your vibrations higher; it makes you aware that you are responsible for attracting all those things that will make your life complete. In other words, have an attitude of gratitude.

Some look at grateful people and say they are lucky or blessed, or just fortunate. But in truth, grateful people simply understand that gratitude is signature strength. They make a point to train their gratitude muscle every day, just as if it were their heart, or their mind, or their body on a treadmill. The result: grateful people have a sense of wonder and look at the world through the eyes of astonishment and joy. By focusing on what they have and being grateful for it, they bypass feelings of neediness, anger, or greediness. All the negativity goes right out the door. I love what this great thinker has to say on the subject:

> *Let us be grateful to people who make us happy—they are the charming gardeners who make our souls blossom.*
>
> —MARCEL PROUST

Be grateful for and bless your qualities and strengths. There is no one else quite like you. Honor and appreciate yourself.

—NINA LESOWITZ
AND MARY BETH SAMMONS

When someone does something well, applaud! You will make two people happy.

—SAMUEL GOLDWYN

He who praises another enriches himself far more than he does the one praised. To praise is an investment in happiness. The poorest human being has something to give that the richest could not buy.

—GEORGE MATTHEW ADAMS

The way to develop the best that is in a man is by appreciation and encouragement.

—CHARLES SCHWAB

Sometimes our light goes out but is blown into flame by another human being. Each of us owes deepest thanks to those who have rekindled this light.

—ALBERT SCHWEITZER

gratitude

_g_

Find the good—and praise it.

—ALEX HALEY

Love your enemy—it will drive him nuts.

—ELEANOR DOAN

True forgiveness is when you can say, "Thank you for that experience."

—OPRAH WINFREY

Cultivate the habit of being grateful for every good thing that comes to you, and give thanks continuously. And because all things have contributed to your advancement, you should include all things in your gratitude.

—RALPH WALDO EMERSON

Let gratitude be the pillow upon which you kneel to say your nightly prayer. And let faith be the bridge you build to overcome evil and welcome good.

—MAYA ANGELOU

Acknowledging the good that you already have in your life is the foundation for all abundance.

—ECKHART TOLLE

If the only prayer you said was thank you, that would be enough.

—MEISTER ECKHART

We must find time to stop and thank the people who make a difference in our lives.

—JOHN F. KENNEDY

You pray in your distress and in your need; would that you might pray also in the fullness of your joy and in your days of abundance.

—KAHLIL GIBRAN

When we give cheerfully and accept gratefully, everyone is blessed.

—MAYA ANGELOU

Some people grumble that roses have thorns; I am grateful that thorns have roses.

—ALPHONSE KARR

Gratitude is not only the greatest of virtues, but the parent of all others.

—MARCUS TULLIUS CICERO

gratitude

We should certainly count our blessings, but we should also make our blessings count.

—NEAL A. MAXWELL

The highest tribute to the dead is not grief but gratitude.

—THORNTON WILDER

Feeling gratitude and not expressing it is like wrapping a present and not giving it.

—WILLIAM ARTHUR WARD

When you rise in the morning, give thanks for the light, for your life, for your strength. Give thanks for your food and for the joy of living. If you see no reason to give thanks, the fault lies in yourself.

—TECUMSEH

The contrast that comes from acknowledging your flaws and imperfections allows for greater compassion, accountability, and gratitude.

—POLLY CAMPBELL

We all know how to say "Thanks." Just saying the word to the barista at your coffee-house, or the guy at the front desk at the gym who swipes your membership card, is a good start. It gives your gratitude muscle a workout and reminds us to thank significant others in our lives as well.

—NINA LESOWITZ
AND MARY BETH SAMMONS

Expressing gratitude is a natural state of being and reminds us that we are all connected.

—VALERIE ELSTER

When you give each other everything, it becomes an even trade. Each wins all.

—LOIS MCMASTER BUJOLD

Happy

Living Every Minute with Love,
Grace, and Gratitude

I LOOK FORWARD each month to *O, The Oprah Maga-zine* and Oprah's ending essay in each issue, "What I Know for Sure." She relates meaningful and profound moments from her life, and often, it can be something that affects us all such as what we all learned from Hurricane Katrina. I am inspired to share things I know for absolutely certain about happiness. Here goes:

- There is enough happiness to go around—it is unlim-ited.
- Kindness and generosity come back to you tenfold.

- You need to have experienced at least some degree of sadness to truly appreciate the opposite.
- Isolating is a surefire way to unhappiness.
- Letting go of emotional baggage is a ticket to more contentedness.
- Holding grudges is useless, wastes time and hurts you more.
- Forgiveness is a high art form, good to practice.
- Having more material belongings is not conducive to happiness.
- Dwelling on the past prevents you from embracing the future.
- Always try and try your best.
- Slowing down increases enjoyment of life immensely.

To get you started, here are some ideas:

C'mon, Get Happy: Ten Ways to Increase Your Happiness Quotient

1) Take a class on something way out of your comfort zone: rock climbing, cooking, photography, pottery, guitar, quilting.

2) Write a poem and send it to a friend you lost touch with.

3) Volunteer at a local preschool (oh, the smiles of children!)

4) Start the day off with a couple of "just catchin' up" calls (instead of Facebooking).

5) Put together a happy CD with the songs that make you happy.

6) Share your happy CD with your five best friends!

7) Take a walk every day after lunch no matter what!

8) Pick a happiness mentor and learn from this master.

9) De-clutter, one area at a time.

10) Organize a regular potluck for pals (I suggest once a week), and each pal takes their turn hosting.

happy

Following all the rules leaves a completed checklist. Following your heart achieves a completed you.

—RAY DAVIS

Know your own happiness. You want nothing but patience—or give it a more fascinating name; call it hope.

—JANE AUSTEN

The happy and efficient people in this world are those who accept trouble as a normal detail of human life and resolve to capitalize it when it comes along.

—H. BERTRAM LEWIS

Happy is he who learns to bear what he cannot change.

—FRIEDERICH SCHILLER

Happiness is having a large, loving, caring, close-knit family in another city.

—GEORGE BURNS

One of the secrets of a happy life is continuous small treats.

—IRIS MURDOCH

Anyone can be happy when times are good; the richer experience is to be happy when times are not.

—SUSAN HARRIS

A happy life is made up of little things…a gift sent, a letter written, a call made, a recommendation given, transportation provided, a cake made, a book lent, a check sent.

—CAROL HOLMES

Do not worry; eat three square meals a day; say your prayers; be courteous to your creditors; keep your digestion good; exercise; go slow and easy. Maybe there are other things your special case requires to make you happy, but my friend, these I reckon will give you a good lift.

—ABRAHAM LINCOLN

Better to be happy than wise.

—JOHN HEYWOOD

Happy the man, and happy he alone, he who can call to-day his own: he who, secure within, can say, to-morrow, do thy worst, for I have liv'd to-day.

—HORACE

Many people think that if they were only in some other place, or had some other job, they would be happy. Well, that is doubtful. So get as much happiness out of what you are doing as you can and don't put off being happy until some future date.

—DALE CARNEGIE

I die—but first I have possess'd, and come what may, I have been bless'd.

—LORD BYRON

Real happiness is cheap enough, yet how dearly we pay for its counterfeit.

—HOSEA BALLOU

Happiness lies in the consciousness we have of it, and by no means in the way the future keeps its promises.

—GEORGE SAND

But earthlier happy is the rose distill'd, than that which withering on the virgin thorn grows, lives and dies in single blessedness.

—WILLIAM SHAKESPEARE

Mankind are always happier for having been happy; so that if you make them happy now, you make them happy twenty years hence by the memory of it.

—SYDNEY SMITH

For it stirs the blood in an old man's heart, and makes his pulses fly, to catch the thrill of a happy voice, and the light of a pleasant eye.

—N. P. WILLIS

True happiness ne'er entered at an eye; true happiness resides in things unseen.

—EDWARD YOUNG

If solid happiness we prize, within our breast this jewel lies, and they are fools who roam; the world has nothing to bestow, from our selves our bliss must flow, and that dear hut, our home.

—NATHANIEL COTTON

A happy life is one spent in learning, earning, and yearning.

—LILLIAN GISH

The greatest part of our happiness depends on our dispositions, not our circumstances.

—MARTHA WASHINGTON

I think happiness is what makes you pretty. Period. Happy people are beautiful. They become like a mirror and they reflect that happiness.

—DREW BARRYMORE

The most important thing is to enjoy your life—to be happy—it's all that matters.

—AUDREY HEPBURN

It is not easy to find happiness in ourselves, and it is not possible to find it elsewhere.

—AGNES REPPLIER

Inspire

The Right Words at the Right Time Will Inspire you to Realize Life's Full Potential

THE INSPIRATION BEHIND the word *inspiration* is the beautiful and ancient Greek concept of taking in the breath of the gods. The Muses, to be specific—nine goddesses who can be called upon by artists, writers or anyone in need of a celestial touch for the creation of art. Of the great Greek poet Homer, author of *The Iliad* and *The Odyssey*, it was said that these great works were inspired in exactly this way. I also love that enthusiasm is thought to come from filling oneself with the very breath of divinity. It makes sense that if you are inspired to write a marvelous novel or poem or get a terrific idea for your next endeavor that you would become enthused, right?

Homer was writing his epic poems in 850 BC and this concept of inspiration has certainly stood the test of time. If anything, the notion of being inspired has only grown and expanded. In the last 3,000 years, it seems at least a few billion people were looking to be filled with the breath of the gods. So, what exactly is it that everyone was looking for?

People wanted to be uplifted, to do great things, help others, make amazing art, leave a legacy and change the world. Just to name a few!

Allen Klein, author of *Inspiration for a Lifetime*, truly inspires me. Here is what he has to say about the subject:

> *The right words at the right time will inspire you to realize life's full potential. Instead of sweating the small stuff, you'll be lifted up and spurred on to tackle life with renewed aplomb.*

The artist has a special task and duty; the task of reminding men of their humanity and the promise of their creativity.

—LEWIS MUMFORD

You are the creature of circumstance or the creator.

—CAVETT ROBERT

You're happiest while you're making the greatest contribution.

—ROBERT F. KENNEDY

You find yourself refreshed by the presence of cheerful people. Why not make an earnest effort to confer that pleasure on others? Half the battle is gained if you never allow yourself to say anything gloomy.

—LYDIA MARIA CHILD

Remember that happiness is as contagious as gloom. It should be the first duty of those who are happy to let others know of their gladness.

—MAURICE MAETERLINCK

Lead the life that will make you kindly and friendly to everyone about you, and you will be surprised what a happy life you will lead.

—CHARLES SCHWAB

When we love, we always strive to become better than we are. When we strive to become better than we are, everything around us becomes better too.

—PAULO COELHO

Sometimes you wake up. Sometimes the fall kills you. And sometimes, when you fall, you fly.

—NEIL GAIMAN

Courage: the most important of all the virtues, because without courage, you can't practice any other virtue consistently.

—MAYA ANGELOU

The things you do for yourself are gone when you are gone, but the things you do for others remain as your legacy.

—KALU NDUKWE KALU

What you do makes a difference, and you have to decide what kind of difference you want to make.

—JANE GOODALL

I was never really insane except upon occasions when my heart was touched.

—EDGAR ALLAN POE

If you treat an individual as he is, he will remain how he is. But if you treat him as if he were what he ought to be and could be, he will become what he ought to be and could be.

—JOHANN WOLFGANG VON GOETHE

To give pleasure to a single heart by a single act is better than a thousand heads bowing in prayer.

—MAHATMA GANDHI

You can't wait for inspiration. You have to go after it with a club.

—JACK LONDON

Your life is an occasion. Rise to it.

—SUZANNE WEYN

It's hard to beat a person who never gives up.

—BABE RUTH

Risks must be taken because the greatest hazard in life is to risk nothing.

—LEO BUSCAGLIA

There is no dishonor in losing the race. There is only dishonor in not racing because you are afraid to lose.

—GARTH STEIN

You have power over your mind—not outside events. Realize this, and you will find strength.

—MARCUS AURELIUS

Every artist makes herself born. You must bring the artist into the world yourself.

—WILLA CATHER

Life is a raw material. We are artisans. We can sculpt our existence into something beautiful, or debase it into ugliness. It's in our hands.

—CATHY BETTER

An inspired life is enjoying and appreciating the journey, whatever it looks like.

—MAYA BAKER

Living your vision offers you the possibility of greater joy, fulfillment, and happiness. And, at best, as you put your stake in the ground for living a more peaceful and loving life, your consciousness generating your actions contributes to the collective consciousness of the Greater Field of Life, and love grows and peace expands for all.

—SUSYN REEVE AND JOAN BREINER

The minute a person whose word means a great deal to others dares to take the openhearted and courageous way, many others follow.

—MARIAN ANDERSON

Joy
This Lovely Lightness of Being

JOY IS AN emotion that bubbles up inside you, an irresistible sensation of happiness that comes upon you unawares. When you hear people talk about this blissful experience, they frequently speak of being filled with joy. I really love the idea of us all being vessels for this feeling of felicity. May our cups runneth over with this lovely lightness of being. Mark Nepo, who happens to be Oprah Winfrey's favorite inspirational writer, has a unique perspective on joy that is utterly fascinating:

Often, what keeps us from joy is the menacing assumption that life is happening other than where we are. So we are always leaving, running from or running to.

What keeps us from joy, then, is often not being where we are and not valuing what is before us.

While happiness is a fleeting mood, joy is larger and more lasting than any one feeling. If each feeling is a wave of emotion, then joy is the ocean that holds all feelings.

Art washes away from the soul the dust of everyday life.

—PABLO PICASSO

Joy, temperance, and repose, slam the door on the doctor's nose.

—HENRY WADSWORTH LONGFELLOW

Man, unlike the animal, has never learned that the sole purpose of life is to enjoy it.

—SAMUEL BUTLER

There is no cure for birth or death save to enjoy the interval.

—GEORGE SANTAYANA

Listen to the clues. The next time you feel real joy, stop and think. Pay attention. Because joy is the universe's way of knocking on your mind's door. Hello in there. Is anyone home? Can I leave a message? Yes? Good! The message is that you are happy, and that means that you are in touch with your purpose.

—STEVE CHANDLER

Joys divided are increased.

—JOSIAH GILBERT HOLLAND

Joy is the feeling of grinning on the inside.

—MELBA COLGROVE

Joy is not in things; it is in us.

—RICHARD WAGNER

Pleasures lie thickest where no pleasures seem; there's not a leaf that falls upon the ground but holds some joy of silence or of sound, some spirit begotten of a summer dream.

—LAMAN BLANCHARD

Live simply. Deepest joy is like a flower... beautiful in essence.

—TONY SAMARA

The joy late coming late departs.

—LEWIS J. BATES

Sweets with sweets war not, joy delights in joy.

—WILLIAM SHAKESPEARE

I have drunken deep of joy, and I will taste no other wine to-night.

—PERCY SHELLEY

Don't cry because it's over, smile because it happened.

—DR. SEUSS

When you do things from your soul, you feel a river moving in you, a joy.

—RUMI

Sometimes your joy is the source of your smile, but sometimes your smile can be the source of your joy.

—THICH NHAT HANH

To get the full value of joy you must have someone to divide it with.

—MARK TWAIN

A thing of beauty is a joy forever.

—JOHN KEATS

Joy is what happens to us when we allow ourselves to recognize how good things really are.

—MARIANNE WILLIAMSON

Joy is to fun what the deep sea is to a puddle. It's a feeling inside that can hardly be contained.

—TERRY PRATCHETT

Life is a Gift—offering us the opportunity to savor, enjoy, celebrate, and honor the mysterious human experience. To continually nourish misery and suffering in our lives diminishes our capacity to truly see and receive the gifts life offers.

—SUSYN REEVE AND JOAN BREINER

I enjoy life when things are happening. I don't care if it's good things or bad things. That means you're alive.

—JOAN RIVERS

Like cliffs worn to their beauty by the pounding of the sea, if we can hold each other up, all that will be left will be wonder and joy.

—MARK NEPO

If a child is to keep alive his inborn sense of wonder, he needs the companionship of at least one adult who can share it, rediscovering with him the joy, excitement and mystery of the world we live in.

—RACHEL CARSON

joy

To be a saint does not exclude fine dresses nor a beautiful house.

—KATHERINE TYNAN HINKSON

Kindness

True Kindness Cannot Be Given Away—It Can Only Be Shared

I AM ONE of the luckiest people on the planet for having the opportunity (and honor) to have worked on the Random Acts of Kindness books and the foundation that sprang from it. What started as a teeny-tiny print run and a few buttons and bumper stickers grew to a million-copy selling phenomenon and a global movement that truly makes the world a better place. Every week, I still hear about Random Acts of Kindness, and it always makes me smile and reminds me to take time out of my busy day and share with others. Kindness is, of course, a virtue and was never more needed than it is today. I believe that one of the reasons Random Acts really took off in this wonderful way is because it is simple, easy and even fun. Nothing feels better than knowing you improved someone's day in some way, be it large or small. We called Will Glennon, the publisher of the books, "Dr Kindness," and I think he certainly deserves an honorary degree for his good works. Here is what he has to say about loving kindness:

> *Kindness is a bottomless fountain—not a river running outward. True kindness cannot be given away, it can only be shared; and in order to share the grace of kindness, we need to partake of it as well. Go out and practice Random Acts of Kindness and you will change the world.*

Kind words can be short and easy to speak, but their echoes are truly endless.

—MOTHER TERESA

The sweetest of all sounds is praise.

—XENOPHON

Every day, tell at least one person something you like, admire, or appreciate about them.

—RICHARD CARLSON

Forgiveness is the way to true health and happiness.

—GERALD JAMPOLSKY

It is more blessed to give than to receive.

—ACTS 20:35

Those who are happiest are those who do the most for others.

—BOOKER T. WASHINGTON

Make people happy and there will not be half the quarreling, or a tenth part of the wickedness there now is.

—LYDIA MARIA CHILD

The happiness of life is made up of minute fractions—the little, soon-forgotten charities of a kiss or smile, a kind look, a heart-felt compliment, and the countless infinitesimals of pleasurable and genial feeling.

—SAMUEL TAYLOR COLERIDGE

The essence of love is kindness.

—ROBERT LOUIS STEVENSON

For attractive lips, speak words of kindness.

—SAM LEVENSON

Be kind, for everyone you meet is fighting a hard battle.

—ATTRIBUTED TO
REVEREND JOHN WATSON

Everytime you smile at someone, it is an action of love, a gift to that person, a beautiful thing.

—MOTHER TERESA

Kindness is a language which the deaf can hear and the blind can see.

—MARK TWAIN

Guard well within yourself that treasure, kindness. Know how to give without hesitation, how to lose without regret, how to acquire without meanness.

—GEORGE SAND

My religion is very simple. My religion is kindness.

—DALAI LAMA XIV

No one has ever become poor by giving.

—ANNE FRANK

I don't feel the slightest interest in the next world; I think it's here. And I think anything good that you're going to do, you should do for other people here and not so you can try to have a happy time in the next world.

—KATHARINE HEPBURN

kindness

The beauty of a woman is not in a facial mole, but true beauty in a woman is reflected in her soul. It is the caring that she lovingly gives, the passion that she knows.

—AUDREY HEPBURN

You cannot do a kindness too soon, for you never know how soon it will be too late.

—RALPH WALDO EMERSON

Tenderness and kindness are not signs of weakness and despair, but manifestations of strength and resolution.

—KAHLIL GIBRAN

I don't think you ever stop giving. I really don't. I think it's an ongoing process. And it's not just about being able to write a check, it's being able to touch somebody's life.

—OPRAH WINFREY

When love and recognition are given with an open heart, our spirits soar and we offer people the opportunity to see themselves through the eyes of those who love and care for them.

—SUSYN REEVE AND JOAN BREINER

I'm an atheist, and that's it. I believe there's nothing we can know except that we should be kind to each other and do what we can for people.

—KATHARINE HEPBURN

Whoever is happy will make others happy too.

—ANNE FRANK

kindness

Love

We Are Meant to Love,
Every Chance We Get

MORE POEMS, PROSE and songs have been devoted to love than any other subject.

Why are we all so in love with love?

Love, whether it is for family, friends or significant others, holds up a mirror in which we see ourselves reflected. It also provides the comfort of connection. People often think they are lucky or unlucky in love. I don't agree with that. I now think love is available to all and there is more than enough for everyone. However, I did not always think that way. A very few years ago, I experienced a great loss when my fiancé passed away and I honestly thought I was off the market when it came to romantic love. I realized that I thought we were all only entitled to one great love per lifetime. I am not sure how I got that idea, but I know I am not the only one with that notion.

I am very lucky to know Judy Ford, a love doctor and top relationship expert (she's also a widow like me.) Her wisdom guided me to a new era and new and more open ways of thinking about love and romance. Thanks to this, I have met the love of my life and have never been happier. We actually read together from Judy's excellent book, *Every Day Love*, which is filled with reminders, both large and small, of how love is something that needs tending. You don't fall in love and remain frozen in time and exactly the same forever. It is really quite the opposite; and a relationship grows and flourishes if it is cherished and cared for. Love is dynamic. But let's have the real expert on love share her insight:

Remember, we are meant to love 24/7. Every chance we get.

—JUDY FORD

Any one reflecting upon the thought he has of the delight, which any present or abstract thing is apt to produce in him, had the idea we call love.

—JOHN LOCKE

Love consists in desiring to give what is our own to another and feeling his delight as our own.

—EMANUEL SWEDENBORG

One word frees us of all the weight and pain of life: that word is love.

—SOPHOCLES

It makes no difference how deeply seated may be the trouble; how hopeless the outlook; how muddled the tangle; how great the mistake. A sufficient realization of love will dissolve it all. If only you could love enough you would be the happiest and most powerful being in the world.

—EMMET FOX

Love is the master key which opens the gates of happiness.

—OLIVER WENDELL HOLMES, SR.

There is only one happiness in life, to love and be loved.

—GEORGE SAND

Love…binds everything together in perfect harmony.

—COLOSSIANS 3:14

True love always brings joy to our self and to the one we love. If our love does not bring joy to both of us, it is not true love.

—THICH NHAT HANH

True love is night jasmine, a diamond in darkness, the heartbeat no cardiologist has ever heard. It is the most common of miracles, fashioned of fleecy clouds—a handful of stars tossed into the night sky.

—JIM BISHOP

You must love yourself before you love another. By accepting yourself and fully being what you are…your simple presence can make others happy.

—JANE ROBERTS

Romance is the glamour which turns the dust of everyday life into a golden haze.

—ELINOR GLYN

When love's well-timed 'tis not a fault to love; the strong, the brave, the virtuous, and the wise, sink in the soft captivity together.

—JOSEPH ADDISON

Love spends his all, and still hath store.

—PHILIP JAMES BAILEY

The sweetest joy, the wildest woe is love.

—PEARL BAILEY

Love looks not with the eyes, but with the mind; and therefore is winged Cupid painted blind.

—WILLIAM SHAKESPEARE

In her first passion woman loves her lover; in all the others, all she loves is love.

—LORD BYRON

Love's too precious to be lost, a little grain shall not be spilt.

—ALFRED, LORD TENNYSON

Till I loved I never lived.

—EMILY DICKINSON

Love consists in desiring to give what is our own to another and feeling his delight as our own.

—EMANUEL SWEDENBORG

Love will make men dare to die for their beloved—love alone; and women as well as men.

—ALEXANDER POPE

It is easy to be loving when the setting is romantic, when you've got extra jingle in your pocket, when you're looking good and feeling fine, but when one of you is out of sorts, exhausted, overwhelmed, and distracted, behaving lovingly requires conscious effort. It's in those moments of restlessness and upheaval that you find out who you are and what it truly means to love each and every day.

—JUDY FORD

It's never too late to fall in love.

—SANDY WILSON

love

I believe every single event in life happens in an opportunity to choose love over fear.

—OPRAH WINFREY

'Tis better to have loved and lost, than never to have loved at all.

—ALFRED, LORD TENNYSON

We cannot really love anybody with whom we never laugh.

—AGNES REPPLIER

Magic

Magic Is Believing in Yourself

THE WORD *MAGIC* comes from an Old Persian word meaning "to be able to have power," why has it become a term associated with children's stories and hogwash tales? Does it still retain any of its old meanings? Although it seems that magic is just a word associated with fantasy, magic is everywhere in our world and still alarmingly powerful. Magic is the many feats mankind accomplishes every day! It's the good that people take part in! Most of all, it is the hope that we all have for a better tomorrow. Just look through all those old children's tales, the ones about dragons and knights and princesses. Those stories are the basis of good vs. evil, the idea that good will always conquer because the good have that magical power in them to continue to hope even through the thickest of moments. Our hope is the only magic we need to push us towards a life of peace and happiness.

Drawing is the discipline by which I constantly rediscover the world. I have learned that what I have not drawn, I have never really seen, and that when I start drawing an ordinary thing, I realize how extraordinary it is, sheer miracle.

—FREDERICK FRANCK

Magic is believing in yourself. If you can do that, you can make anything happen.

—JOHANN WOLFGANG VON GOETHE

I have always been delighted at the prospect of a new day, a fresh try, one more start, with perhaps a bit of magic waiting somewhere behind the morning.

—J. B. PRIESTLEY

Of all of our inventions for mass communication, pictures still speak the most universally understood language.

—WALT DISNEY

Music is the strongest form of magic.

—MARILYN MANSON

There is a real magic in enthusiasm. It spells the difference between mediocrity and accomplishment.

—NORMAN VINCENT PEALE

Imagination is the true magic carpet.

—NORMAN VINCENT PEALE

If you can dream it, you can do it.

—WALT DISNEY

Love and magic have a great deal in common. They enrich the soul, delight the heart, and they both take practice.

—NORA ROBERTS

Mystery is the basic appeal of magic. Once the secrets are known, the magician becomes a mere manipulator, an actor in a suspense drama which has little impact because the audience knows the ending in advance.

—CHRISTOPHER MILBOURNE

I don't want realism. I want magic!

—TENNESSEE WILLIAMS

Magic becomes art when it has nothing to hide.

—BEN OKRI

There is magic, but you have to be the magician. You have to make the magic happen.

—SIDNEY SHELDON

That's the thing with magic. You've got to know it's still here, all around us, or it just stays invisible for you.

—CHARLES DE LINT

A magician is strong because he feels pain. He feels the difference between what the world is and what he would make of it.

—LEV GROSSMAN

We do not need magic to transform our world. We carry all of the power we need inside ourselves already.

—J. K. ROWLING

Magic can be found in stolen moments.

—FRANCESCA LIA BLOCK

And above all, watch with glittering eyes the whole world around you because the greatest secrets are always hidden in the most unlikely places. Those who don't believe in magic will never find it.

—ROALD DAHL

Disbelief in magic can force a poor soul into believing in government and business.

—TOM ROBBINS

The world is full of magic things, patiently waiting for our senses to grow sharper.

—W. B. YEATS

Creativity is a sacred universal energy, a manifestation of the divine.

—ADRIANA DIAZ

Our lives themselves are the ultimate act of creativity, and each of our lives is as unique as our fingerprints.

—MAGGIE OMAN SHANNON

I believe in pink. I believe that laughing is the best calorie burner. I believe in kissing, kissing a lot. I believe in being strong when everything seems to be going wrong. I believe that happy girls are the prettiest girls. I believe that tomorrow is another day and I believe in miracles.

—AUDREY HEPBURN

When you're around kids you can be a little kid yourself and pretend that life is magic and you don't have to be one of those sweaty people going to work every day.

—AMY WINEHOUSE

Infinity is present in each part. A loving smile contains all art. The motes of starlight spark and dart. A grain of sand holds power and might.

—MADELEINE L'ENGLE

Nostalgia

Cherish All Your Happy Moments

WE'RE ALWAYS LOOKING back on the old days and wondering why we took them for granted so often. Why didn't I dance more when I was young? Why didn't I go out more? Why didn't I ever find my calling or find something I was truly passionate about? But looking back on it all weren't there times you laughed? Times you loved? Times you were *so* passionate it felt like the world would end? Of course we took it for granted! We still take every day in the present for granted! It's because we never feel for something as much as when it's gone. Absence makes the heart grow fonder, even absence of times you thought

n

you were glad to get rid of, like the ever-antagonizing high school years. The choice is yours, whether to embrace the happiness of having nostalgia or whether to dwell on it as an escape from the present. Use nostalgia to fuel your desire to make better memories for the future you to look back on!

> *I can only note that the past is beautiful because one never realizes an emotion at the time. It expands later, and thus we don't have complete emotions about the present, only about the past.*
>
> —VIRGINIA WOOLF

The happiest moments of my life have been the few which I have passed at home in the bosom of my family.

—THOMAS JEFFERSON

Youth! Stay close to the young and a little rubs off.

—ALAN JAY LERNER

Those who love the young best stay younger longer.

—EDGAR FRIEDENBERG

The great man is he that does not lose his child-heart.

—MENCIUS

So, like a forgotten fire, a childhood can always flare up again within us.

—GASTON BACHELARD

Cherish all your happy moments; they make a fine cushion for old age.

—BOOTH TARKINGTON

Bliss was it in that dawn to be alive, but to be young was very heaven.

—WILLIAM WORDSWORTH

How often have I lain beneath rain on a strange roof, thinking of home.

—WILLIAM FAULKNER

The times you lived through, the people you shared those times with—nothing brings it all to life like an old mix tape. It does a better job of storing up memories than actual brain tissue can do. Every mix tape tells a story. Put them together, and they can add up to the story of a life.

—ROB SHEFFIELD

Nostalgia is a necessary thing, I believe, and a way for all of us to find peace in that which we have accomplished, or even failed to accomplish.

—R. A. SALVATORE

There is something incredibly nostalgic and significant about the annual cascade of autumn leaves.

—JOE L. WHEELER

There are a few moments in your life when you are truly and completely happy, and you remember to give thanks. Even as it happens you are nostalgic for the moment, you are tucking it away in your scrapbook.

—DAVID BENIOFF

Philosophy is really nostalgia, the desire to be at home.

—NOVALIS

There are no days more full than those we go back to.

—COLUM MCCANN

Nostalgia is like a grammar lesson: you find the present tense, and the past perfect!

—OWENS LEE POMEROY

When I'm eighty years old and sitting in my rocking chair, I'll be reading Harry Potter. And my family will say to me, "After all this time?" And I will say, "Always."

—ALAN RICKMAN

Ever poised on that cusp between past and future, we tie memories to souvenirs like string to trees along life's path, marking the trail in case we lose ourselves around a bend of tomorrow's road.

—SUSAN LENDROTH

Nostalgia is the only friend that stays with you forever.

—DAMIEN ECHOLS

We could never have loved the earth so well if we had had no childhood in it.

—GEORGE ELIOT

One is always at home in one's past...

—VLADIMIR NABOKOV

To be honest, I think kids have got a lot more going on than adults. They've got their heads screwed on a lot better.

—AMY WINEHOUSE

The great thing about getting older is that you don't lose all the other ages you've been.

—MADELEINE L'ENGLE

"Home" is any four walls that enclose the right person.

—HELEN ROWLAND

nostalgia

At midlife I'm having to recognize that there are people I may never be reconciled with. People I loved dearly but we went as far as we could go together. We loved; we tried; that may have been enough.

—ZANA

During my long crisis, my genius, the animus, the male part of the female soul, that assists the female artist, had abandoned me.... But at the beginning of the fifties, I sensed that things were getting better.

—MERET OPPENHEIM

Open-Minded

Let Your Interests Be as Wide as Possible

"IGNORANCE IS BLISS" is a true statement, but is often misused. Ignorance caused by one *choosing* not to accept or try to understand something leads only to prejudice and anger, not happiness. But choosing to be open-minded towards something you don't understand might lead to a love of something new and wholly unexpected! The mind was built to *learn* and continuously desires to decipher the world it sees around it. It doesn't mean you have to accept *everything* for what it is, or love everything even though we might find it distasteful—as long as we give things a chance, give our mind a moment to conceptualize what it sees, before closing it off and assuming what it does not know. Listen to a new style of music for an hour, go hiking, read a biography of someone you always believed strange—find *something* every day to open your mind to, and you're guaranteed to find something that will make you happy now and then.

My mind to me a kingdom is; such present joys therein I find that it excels all other bliss that earth affords or grows by kind.

—EDWARD DYER

Learning to draw is really a matter of learning to see—to see correctly—and that means a good deal more than merely looking with the eye.

—KIMON NICOLAIDES

I shut my eyes in order to see.

—PAUL GAUGUIN

Seek the wisdom of the ages, but look at the world through the eyes of a child.

—RON WILD

The secret of happiness is this: let your interests be as wide as possible, and let your reactions to things and persons that interest you be as far as possible friendly rather than hostile.

—BERTRAND RUSSELL

open-minded

The way to happiness: keep your heart free from hate, your mind from worry. Live simply, expect little, give much. Fill your life with love. Scatter sunshine. Forget self, think of others. Do as you would be done by. Try this for a week and you will be surprised.

—NORMAN VINCENT PEALE

Prosperity is not without many fears and distastes, and adversity is not without comforts and hopes.

—FRANCIS BACON

The earth was made so various, that the mind of desultory man, studious of change and pleased with novelty, might be indulged.

—WILLIAM COWPER

A mind is like a parachute. It doesn't work if it is not open.

—FRANK ZAPPA

Those who cannot change their minds cannot change anything.

—GEORGE BERNARD SHAW

It is never too late to give up your prejudices.

—HENRY DAVID THOREAU

Let yourself be open and life will be easier. A spoon of salt in a glass of water makes the water undrinkable. A spoon of salt in a lake is almost unnoticed.

—SIDDHARTHA GAUTAMA BUDDHA

Begin challenging your own assumptions. Your assumptions are your windows on the world. Scrub them off every once in awhile, or the light won't come in.

—ALAN ALDA

The mind that opens to a new idea never returns to its original size.

—ALBERT EINSTEIN

The thing is, it's very dangerous to have a fixed idea. A person with a fixed idea will always find some way of convincing himself in the end that he is right.

—ATLE SELBERG

open-minded

Truth is, I'll never know all there is to know about you just as you will never know all there is to know about me. Humans are by nature too complicated to be understood fully. So we can choose either to approach our fellow human beings with suspicion or to approach them with an open mind, a dash of optimism and a great deal of candor.

—TOM HANKS

They are ill discoverers that think there is no land when they can see nothing but sea.

—FRANCIS BACON

Flexibility requires an open mind and a welcoming of new alternatives.

—DEBORAH DAY

Some people like living in black and white worlds. Let them stay there. Appreciate all the colors you see in your world though.

—ASHLY LORENZANA

We must quit thinking we know everything, and quit placing "knowledge" over kindness and compassion.

—BRYANT MCGILL

I have no methods; all I do is accept people as they are.

—JOAN RIVERS

Sometimes you can't see yourself clearly until you see yourself through the eyes of others.

—ELLEN DEGENERES

One way to open your eyes is to ask yourself, "What if I had never seen this before? What if I knew I would never see it again?"

—RACHEL CARSON

If the bird does like its cage, and *does* like its sugar, and will not leave it, why keep the door so very carefully shut?

—OLIVE SCHREINER

I learned to make my mind large, as the universe is large, so that there is room for paradoxes.

—MAXINE HONG KINGSTON

Purpose

Find Your Purpose and Give Your Whole Heart and Soul to It

THE PHRASE "purpose of life" is a paradox in itself. Life—living and enjoying the little time you have on this earth—is the purpose! Happiness is the purpose! There is usually little purpose in you being here, since most of us are here by accident, but to make or find our purpose in life, we must find a *reason* to live. It may be our family, it may be our job or duty to the world, it may be our lover or it may just be the pure joy in seeing the nature of the world, and seizing the many possibilities of happiness in our lives; whatever it is, we must find our reason for existing in order to understand our purpose in life.

Learn to get in touch with the silence within yourself and know that everything in this life has a purpose. There are no mistakes, no coincidences, all events are blessings given to us to learn from.

—ELISABETH KÜBLER-ROSS

The purpose of life is a life of purpose.

—ROBERT BYRNE

The grand essentials to happiness in this life are something to do, something to love, and something to hope for.

—JOSEPH ADDISON

It is a man's proper business to seek happiness and avoid misery.

—JOHN LOCKE

Happiness is the meaning and the purpose of life, the whole aim and end of human existence.

—ARISTOTLE

Nothing can bring you peace but yourself. Nothing can bring you peace but the triumph of principles.

—RALPH WALDO EMERSON

Your purpose in life is to find your purpose and give your whole heart and soul to it.

—ANONYMOUS

We live in deeds, not years; in thoughts, not breaths; in feelings, not in figures on a dial. We should count time by heart-throbs. He most lives who thinks most, feels the noblest, acts the best.

—PHILIP JAMES BAILEY

He who has a why to live for can bear almost any how.

—FRIEDRICH NIETZSCHE

The purpose of life is not to be happy. It is to be useful, to be honorable, to be compassionate, to have it make some difference that you have lived and lived well.

—RALPH WALDO EMERSON

A man said to the universe: "Sir, I exist!" "However," replied the universe, "the fact has not created in me a sense of obligation."

—STEPHEN CRANE

All of us have a place in history. Mine is clouds.

—RICHARD BRAUTIGAN

If you want to accomplish the goals of your life, you have to begin with the spirit.

—OPRAH WINFREY

If you were all alone in the universe with no one to talk to, no one with which to share the beauty of the stars, to laugh with, to touch, what would be your purpose in life? It is other life; it is love, which gives your life meaning. This is harmony. We must discover the joy of each other, the joy of challenge, the joy of growth.

—MITSUGI SAOTOME

Here is a test to find out whether your mission in life is complete. If you're alive, it isn't.

—LAUREN BACALL

Make your work to be in keeping with your purpose.

—LEONARDO DA VINCI

Great minds have purpose, others have wishes. Little minds are tamed and subdued by misfortunes; but great minds rise above them.

—WASHINGTON IRVING

purpose

You are here in order to enable the world to live more amply, with greater vision, with a finer spirit of hope and achievement. You are here to enrich the world.

—WOODROW WILSON

We may run, walk, stumble, drive, or fly, but let us never lose sight of the reason for the journey, or miss a chance to see a rainbow on the way.

—GLORIA GAITHER

Find the thing you want to do most intensely, make sure that's it, and do it with all your might. If you live, well and good. If you die, well and good. Your purpose is done.

—H. G. WELLS

It's not enough to have lived. We should be determined to live for something.

—WINSTON CHURCHILL

Keep your eyes and ears open. Opportunity is everywhere, if you're alert enough to recognize it.

—BJ GALLAGHER

You have to do what you love to do, not get stuck in that comfort zone of a regular job. Life is not a dress rehearsal. This is it.

—LUCINDA BASSETT

The biggest adventure you can take is to live the life of your dreams.

—OPRAH WINFREY

Those who have failed to work toward the truth have missed the purpose of living.

—SIDDHARTHA GAUTAMA BUDDHA

The trick is to feel that something you do can be useful to someone else, whether for pleasure or for pay. In my eyes, everyone has a talent of one kind or another. You might tell a good story. You might be a genius at math. Talent doesn't mean creative expression, nor does it mean star-quality fame.

—PAULA SNYDER

purpose

Quintessence (of Life)

The Fifth and Highest
Element of Happiness

IN PHILOSOPHY, IT is the fifth and highest element that permeates all of nature. In physics, it is much the same and is proposed to be the fifth fundamental force, or a form of dark energy that accelerates the expansion of the universe. Whether or not it is the meaning of life, the quintessence, or highest element of happiness, is the form of happiness we all desire. It is a pure happiness that comes from within *and* without and is undaunted by the evil and negative things in the world and in ourselves. It is that otherness in the world that only comes from peace and united joy. Although this seems absolutely unattainable, that doesn't mean we should give up hope. Hope guides mankind to do great things, and although ultimate and pure happiness seems impossible, it doesn't mean that it shouldn't be strived for. Even if you are alone in your search for it, if you strive for the quintessence of happiness in life, then in return, won't you become the quintessence of your own being? You would be the ideal you!

The earth is the very quintessence of the human condition.

—HANNAH ARENDT

A man's best things are nearest him, lie close about his feet.

—RICHARD MONCKETON MILNES

Love brings to light a lover's noble and hidden qualities—his rare and exceptional traits: it is thus liable to be deceptive of his normal qualities.

—FRIEDRICH NIETZSCHE

Love is the ultimate creator.

—MOLLY FRIEDENFELD

The only way you can be the best at something is to be the best you can be.

—SUSAN BETH PFEFFER

In essence, we are deeper than being; we are character, which contains the conscious forces of love, justice, kindness, faith, and forgiveness.

—GAREY GORDON

quintessence (of life)

q
————

There is a light in this world, a healing spirit more powerful than any darkness we may encounter. We sometimes lose sight of this force when there is suffering, too much pain. Then suddenly, the spirit will emerge through the lives of ordinary people who hear a call and answer in extraordinary ways.

—MOTHER TERESA

You've gotta dance like there's nobody watching, love like you'll never be hurt, sing like there's nobody listening, and live like it's heaven on earth.

—WILLIAM W. PURKEY

I think heaven will be like a first kiss.

—SARAH ADDISON ALLEN

Perfection is achieved, not when there is nothing more to add, but when there is nothing left to take away.

—ANTOINE DE SAINT-EXUPÉRY

I'm living a dream I never want to wake up from.

—CRISTIANO RONALDO

Too late, I found you can't wait to become perfect, you got to go out and fall down and get up with everybody else.

—RAY BRADBURY

Perfection is not a destination, it's a never-ending process...enjoy!

—JIM BOUCHARD

Courage: the most important of all the virtues, because without courage, you can't practice any other virtue consistently.

—MAYA ANGELOU

The energy of the mind is the essence of life.

—ARISTOTLE

Living is about capturing the essence of things.

—C. JOYBELL C

The true perfection of man lies not in what man has, but in what man is.

—OSCAR WILDE

quintessence (of life)

The essence of any creature encompasses more than one realm. Here now this body is a vehicle of my essence in this universe.

—TOBA BETA

The true essence of who you are balances itself upon a cushion of purity, benevolence, and holiness.

—GAREY GORDON

A man is relieved and gay when he has put his heart into his work and done his best.

—RALPH WALDO EMERSON

Beauty is about being comfortable in your own skin. It's about knowing and accepting who you are.

—ELLEN DEGENERES

I never lose sight of the fact that just being is fun.

—KATHARINE HEPBURN

Your purpose on earth is to evolve to your highest possible state of being.

—TONY BURROUGHS

Sooner or later we all discover that the important moments in life are not the advertised ones, not the birthdays, the graduations, the weddings, not the great goals achieved. The real milestones are less prepossessing. They come to the door of memory unannounced, stray dogs that amble in, sniff around a bit and simply never leave. Our lives are measured by these.

—SUSAN B. ANTHONY

Oh, never mind the fashion. When one has a style of one's own, it is always twenty times better.

—MARGARET OLIPHANT

Relax

Doing Nothing:
It Brings a Fresh Perspective

OF COURSE YOU have to be active and persistent in order to pursue happiness, but you also have to let yourself relax and enjoy life too. It can be really hard to allow yourself to relax these days, what with being tethered to one electronic device or another, but each one of us must force ourselves to set that cell phone down and close our laptops, because without turning off our devices and resting our mind and body, how can we ever expect ourselves to think properly?

Relaxation is an art that has been made very difficult to practice by the conditions of modern civilization.

—ALANIS MORISSETTE

Constant distractions from peace of mind can lead to constant stress. It may seem like only the busiest people succeed, but the busiest and constantly stressed out people also fall the hardest. Remember, Rome wasn't built in a day! The ancient Romans used to take siesta every day after lunch because they knew the importance of rest for success. If the most powerful empire of all time could still relax in the wake of constant power, then why can't you?

Don't forget the famous song by Frankie Goes to Hollywood! Listen to Frankie, and relax, because you have all of life to "go to it" and build your empire of happiness!

If you can spend a perfectly useless after-noon in a perfectly useless manner, you have learned how to live.

—LIN YUTANG

If we could learn how to balance rest against effort, calmness against strain, quiet against turmoil, we would assure ourselves of joy in living and psychological health for life.

—JOSEPHINE RATHBONE

When we feel joyful, euphoric, happy, we are more open to life, more capable of seeing things clearly and handling daily tensions.

—LEO BUSCAGLIA

Happiness is a butterfly, which, when pursued, is always just beyond your grasp, but which, if you will sit down quietly, may alight upon.

—NATHANIEL HAWTHORNE

Ah! There is nothing like staying at home, for real comfort.

—JANE AUSTEN

It's a good idea always to do something relaxing prior to making an important decision in your life.

—PAULO COELHO

Just breathing can be such a luxury sometimes.

—WALTER KIRN

It's better to oversleep and miss the boat than get up early and sink.

—ELIZABETH JANE HOWARD

Just relax. Everyone around you is working too hard.

—BAUVARD

Turn off your mind, relax, and float downstream.

—JOHN LENNON

There are times when we stop, we sit still. We listen and breezes from a whole other world begin to whisper.

—JAMES CARROL

I think best in a hot bath, with my head tilted back and my feet up high.

—ELIZABETH JANE HOWARD

relax

On every mountain height is rest.

—JOHANN WOLFGANG VON GOETHE

Rest is not quitting the busy career, rest is the fitting of self to its sphere.

—JOHN S. DWIGHT

Rest is sweet after strife.

—OWEN MEREDITH

And rest, that strengthens unto virtuous deeds, is one with prayer.

—BAYARD TAYLOR

Now is done thy long day's work; fold thy palms across thy breast, fold thine arms, turn to thy rest. Let them rave.

—ALFRED, LORD TENNYSON

Thou hadst, for weary feet, the gift of rest.

—WILLIAM WATSON

Your mind will answer most questions if you learn to relax and wait for the answer.

—ROBERT A. HEINLEIN

Saturday is a day for the spa. RELAX, indulge, enjoy, and love yourself, too.

—ANA MONNAR

Breathe. Let go. And remind yourself that this very moment is the only one you know you have for sure.

—OPRAH WINFREY

Procrastination is not the problem. It is the solution. It is the universe's way of saying stop, slow down, you move too fast. Listen to the music. Whoa whoa, listen to the music. Because music makes the people come together, it makes the bourgeois and the rebel.

—ELLEN DEGENERES

To achieve the impossible dream, try going to sleep.

—JOAN KLEMPNER

Interrupt your daily routine on a weekend by doing *nothing*; it brings a fresh perspective.

—CAROL WISEMAN

If you realize too acutely how valuable time is, you are too paralyzed to do anything.

—KATHARINE BUTLER HATHAWAY

relax

Silly

Life's Better when It's Fun

THE DICTIONARIES DEFINE *silly* as someone who is lacking common sense and foolish, but I've always believed that you need to be silly throughout life in order to retain any sense or sanity. In every laugh is a smile—the ultimate symbol of happiness.

There was a time when I was traveling abroad with my best friend Nick; in the middle of our two months of backpacking across Europe, we were broke, tired, nearly disabled by injuries, surrounded by several stray dogs and sleeping on the dim and dodgy streets of the port of Athens, Greece. I felt like my spirits could never be raised

S out of the depths of the hells we had to face. But just when I had begun to think of going home and ending our adventures, Nick was the silly savior to the rescue! His jokes and foolishness kept me smiling and laughing the whole evening, and to this day I smile every time I think about the crazy night we spent on the streets of Athens.

So never frown on silliness, because it might just turn the most miserable of memories into the fondest.

I believe we should all pay our tax bill with a smile. I tried—but they wanted cash.

—ANONYMOUS

Life's better when it's fun. Boy, that's deep, isn't it?

—KEVIN COSTNER

Laugh. Laugh as much as you can. Laugh until you cry. Cry until you laugh.

—ELLEN DEGENERES

Humor is the healthy way of feeling "distance" between one's self and the problem, a way of standing off and looking at one's problems with perspective.

—ROLLO MAY

Humor has a great power to heal on an emotional level. You can't hold anger, you can't hold fear, you can't hold hurt while you're laughing.

—STEVE BHAERMAN
(A.K.A. SWAMI BEYONDANANDA)

Humor enables one to live in the midst of tragic events without becoming a tragic figure.

—E. T. "CY" EBERHART

You should never assume. You know what happens when you assume. You make an ass out of you and me because that's how it's spelled.

—ELLEN DEGENERES

God is a comedian whose audience is afraid to laugh.

—H. L. MENCKEN

It has always seemed to me that hearty laughter is a good way to jog internally without having to go outdoors.

—NORMAN COUSINS

A good belly laugh is like taking your liver for a horseback ride.

—BONNY CLARK

Happiness is a warm puppy.

—CHARLES M. SCHULZ

Old friends are best. King James used to call for his old shoes; they were easiest for his feet.

—JOHN SELDEN

The soul's calm sunshine, and the heartfelt joy, is virtue's prize.

—ALEXANDER POPE

A little nonsense now and then is cherished by the wisest men.

—ROALD DAHL

There's nothing like deep breaths after laughing that hard. Nothing in the world like a sore stomach for the right reasons.

—STEPHEN CHBOSKY

One of the keys to happiness is a bad memory.

—RITA MAE BROWN

With mirth and laughter let old wrinkles come.

—WILLIAM SHAKESPEARE

It's a helluva start, being able to recognize what makes you happy.

—LUCILLE BALL

My advice to you is not to inquire why or whither, but just enjoy your ice cream while it's on your plate.

—THORNTON WILDER

Life doesn't make any sense, and we all pretend it does. Comedy's job is to point out that it doesn't make sense, and that it doesn't make much difference anyway.

—ERIC IDLE

Procrastinate now, don't put it off.

—ELLEN DEGENERES

There is always something to chuckle about. Sometimes we see it. Sometimes...we don't. Still, the world is filled with humor. It is there when we are happy and it is there to cheer us up when we are not.

—ALLEN KLEIN

Many search for happiness as we look for a hat we wear on our heads.

—NIKOLAUS LENUS

Whoever said money can't buy happiness simply didn't know where to go shopping.

—BO DEREK

Humor is just truth, only faster.

—GILDA RADNER

Thoughtful

The Happiness of Your Life Depends Upon the Quality of Your Thoughts

YOUR BODY MAY be the temple, but your mind is the heavens above which your body must follow; only good thoughts lead to good actions. Noetic science has made many breakthroughs in the past years in discovering the true effectiveness of thoughts on the physical world. A large amount of good thoughts have been said to influence physical things in a beneficial way, from the orderly and beautiful formation of ice crystals to the healing of bodies riddled with cancer and other illnesses. Good intentions *do* benefit your life and the lives of others, and being thoughtful and having the intention for good influences the world around you. Harness your thoughts for good and let the negative thoughts that come to you wash away. Try to understand the world and all the good that it holds in order to think well of it. Being thoughtful both in mind and action will benefit your world and is your greatest tool for ultimate happiness.

The happiness of your life depends upon the quality of your thoughts.

—MARCUS ANTONIUS

When ill luck besets us, to ease the tension we have only to remember that happiness is relative. The next time you are tempted to grumble about what has happened to you, why not pause and be glad that it is no worse than it is?

—DALE CARNEGIE

We are never so happy nor so unhappy as we imagine.

—FRANÇOIS DE LA ROCHEFOUCAULD

You have to believe in happiness, or happiness never comes.

—DOUGLAS MALLOCH

The weak can never forgive. Forgiveness is the attribute of the strong.

—MAHATMA GANDHI

Wrinkles should merely indicate where smiles have been.

—MARK TWAIN

Why should we refuse the happiness this hour gives us, because some other hour might take it away?

—JOHN OLIVER HOBBES

When we align our thoughts, emotions, and actions with the highest part of ourselves, we are filled with enthusiasm, purpose, and meaning…. We are joyously and intimately engaged with our world. This is the experience of authentic power.

—GARY ZUKAV

A cheerful temper joined with innocence will make beauty attractive, knowledge delightful, and wit good natured.

—JOSEPH ADDISON

Life is but thought, so think I will.

—WILLIAM TAYLOR COLERIDGE

Still are the thoughts to memory dear.

—SIR WALTER SCOTT

Thought alone is eternal.

—OWEN MEREDITH

The revelation of thought takes men out of servitude into freedom.

—RALPH WALDO EMERSON

Our growing thought makes growing revelation.

—GEORGE ELIOT

They are never alone that are accompanied with noble thoughts.

—SIR PHILIP SIDNEY

Their cause I plead—plead it in heart and in mind; a fellow-feeling makes one wondrous kind.

—DAVID GARRICK

Happiness is when what you think, what you say, and what you do are in harmony.

—MAHATMA GANDHI

On that best portion of a good man's life, his little, nameless, unremembered acts of kindness and love.

—WILLIAM WORDSWORTH

Humility is not thinking less of yourself, it's thinking of yourself less.

—C.S. LEWIS

Creative minds have always been known to survive any kind of bad training.

—ANNA FREUD

Everything in your world—the world at large, as well as your individual world, including everything you see, hear, smell, taste, touch, and feel—is the result of a thought manifestation.

—TONY BURROUGHS

Look at your feet. You are standing in the sky. When we think of the sky, we tend to look up, but the sky actually begins at the earth.

—DIANE ACKERMAN

Great men are they who see that spiritual is stronger than any material force, that thoughts rule the world.

—RALPH WALDO EMERSON

Those who contemplate the beauty of the earth find reserves of strength that will endure as long as life lasts.

—RACHEL CARSON

Never doubt that a small group of thoughtful, committed citizens can change the world. Indeed, it is the only thing that ever has.

—MARGARET MEAD

thoughtful

Understanding
What the World Needs Now

THE ABILITY TO understand each other's sufferings and actions is the key to coexistence and happiness for all. As youths, most of us are unhappy, wallowing in self-pity and frustrated at the world for not understanding us. We lash out because we cannot look at anything but our own misery. As we get older, we realize that it's not the world misunderstanding us, it's us not understanding the world. We learn to open our eyes and see that the world doesn't revolve around us, and begin to see that the world needs more understanding and compassion than we do. Opening ourselves up to understanding the world as it is and as it could be will lead to progress towards happiness for all, and will give happiness to the self as well.

All that is good in art is the expression of one soul talking to another, and is precious according to the greatness of the soul that utters it.

—JOHN RUSKIN

Children, like animals, use all their senses to discover the world. Then artists come along and discover it the same way all over again.

—EUDORA WELTY

The parent exists to teach the child, but also they must learn what the child has to teach them; and the child has a very great deal to teach them.

—ARNOLD BENNETT

True happiness is to understand our duties towards God and man; to enjoy the present, without anxious dependence on the future, not to amuse ourselves with either hopes or fears, but to rest satisfied with what we have, which is abundantly sufficient.

—SENECA

But what is happiness except the simple harmony between a man and the life he leads?

—ALBERT CAMUS

Peace rules the day, where reason rules the mind.

—WILKIE COLLINS

Not chaos-like together crush'd and bruis'd, but, as the world, harmoniously confused; where order in variety we see, and where, though all things differ, all agree.

—ALEXANDER POPE

The secrets of life are not shown except to sympathy and likeness.

—RALPH WALDO EMERSON

We are addicted to our thoughts. We cannot change anything if we cannot change our thinking.

—SANTOSH KALWAR

Any fool can know. The point is to understand.

—ALBERT EINSTEIN

You are, after all, what you think. Your emotions are the slaves to your thoughts, and you are the slave to your emotions.

—ELIZABETH GILBERT

Everything that irritates us about others can lead us to an understanding of ourselves.

—CARL JUNG

Try to understand men. If you understand each other, you will be kind to each other. Knowing a man well never leads to hate and almost always leads to love.

—JOHN STEINBECK

One of the tasks of true friendship is to listen compassionately and creatively to the hidden silences. Often secrets are not revealed in words, they lie concealed in the silence between the words or in the depth of what is unsayable between two people.

—JOHN O'DONOHUE

Those who know, do. Those that understand, teach.

—ANONYMOUS

If you know the why, you can live any how.

—FRIEDRICH NIETZSCHE

Because it's no longer enough to be a decent person. It's no longer enough to shake our heads and make concerned grimaces at the news. True enlightened activism is the only thing that can save humanity from itself.

—JOSS WHEDON

The world has a soul and whoever understands that soul can also understand the language of many things.

—PAULO COELHO

Be the one who nurtures and builds. Be the one who has an understanding and a forgiving heart; one who looks for the best in people. Leave people better than you found them.

—MARVIN J. ASHTON

We all live with the objective of being happy; our lives are all different and yet the same.

—ANNE FRANK

Understanding that the right to choose your own path is a sacred privilege. Use it. Dwell in possibility.

—OPRAH WINFREY

Find out who you are and figure out what you believe in. Even if it's different from what your neighbors believe in and different from what your parents believe in. Stay true to yourself. Have your own opinion. Don't worry about what people say about you or think about you. Let the naysayers nay. They will eventually grow tired of naying.

—ELLEN DEGENERES

There is no way in which to understand the world without first detecting it through the radar net of our senses.

—DIANE ACKERMAN

understanding

To stand at the edge of the sea, to sense the ebb and flow of the tides, to feel the breath of a mist moving over a great salt marsh, to watch the flight of shore birds that have swept up and down the surf lines of the continents for untold thousands of years, to see the running of the old eels and the young shad to the sea, is to have knowledge of things that are as nearly eternal as any earthly life can be.

—RACHEL CARSON

Vivacious

Lust for Life

GINGER ROGERS, KNOWN for her dancing, her exciting
flair and of course that smile that seems to bring the
world back to life every time I see it, is the embodiment
of vivaciousness—so it was no wonder they chose her for
the title character in the 1938 hit movie *Vivacious Lady*.
A cutting-edge kind of woman, a nightclub singer who is
fun, adventurous and always following her heart, Ginger's
character Francey is someone to aspire to emulate. She
lives life and she's not afraid of anyone she has to fight to
enjoy it. James Stewart's character Peter Morgan falls in
love with Francey, and so did the rest of the world. Full of

life and happy to be so, Francey is hard not to fall in love with—see the movie for yourself and just you try!

The artist is the confidant of nature; flowers carry on dialogues with him through the graceful bending of their stems and the harmoniously tinted nuances of their blossoms. Every flower has a cordial word which nature directs towards him.

—AUGUSTE RODIN

There are painters who transform the sun to a yellow spot, but there are others who, with the help of their art and their intelligence, transform a yellow spot into a sun.

—PABLO PICASSO

Science and art have in common that everyday things seem to them new and attractive.

—FRIEDRICH NIETZSCHE

Do not dwell in the past, do not dream of the future, concentrate the mind on the present moment.

—ANONYMOUS

In three words I can sum up everything I've learned about life: it goes on.

—ROBERT FROST

When I stand before God at the end of my life, I would hope that I would not have a single bit of talent left, and I could say, "I used everything you gave me."

—ERMA BOMBECK

Believe that life is worth living and your belief will help create the fact.

—WILLIAM JAMES

You will never be happy if you continue to search for what happiness consists of. You will never live if you are looking for the meaning of life.

—ALBERT CAMUS

All life is an experiment. The more experiments you make the better.

—RALPH WALDO EMERSON

We inter-breathe with the rain forests, we drink from the oceans. They are part of our own body.

—THICH NHAT HANH

You didn't come into this world. You came out of it, like a wave from the ocean. You are not a stranger here.

—ALAN WATTS

I am in love with this world...I have climbed its mountains, roamed its forests, sailed its waters, crossed its deserts, felt the sting of its frosts, the oppression of its heats, the drench of its rains, the fury of its winds, and always have beauty and joy waited upon my goings and comings.

—JOHN BURROUGHS

In those vernal seasons of the year, when the air is calm and pleasant, it were an injury and sullenness against Nature not to go out and see her riches, and partake in her rejoicing with heaven and earth.

—JOHN MILTON

And forget not that the earth delights to feel your bare feet and the winds long to play with your hair.

—KAHLIL GIBRAN

Do something to renew and revive *you*.

—CAROLE BRODY FLEET

Look! Look! Look deep into nature and you will understand everything.

—ALBERT EINSTEIN

As long as I live, I'll hear waterfalls and birds and winds sing. I'll interpret the rocks, learn the language of flood, storm, and the avalanche. I'll acquaint myself with the glaciers and wild gardens, and get as near the heart of the world as I can.

—JOHN MUIR

The purpose of life is undoubtedly to know oneself. We cannot do it unless we learn to identify ourselves with all that lives. The sum-total of that life is God.

—MAHATMA GANDHI

It's kind of fun to do the impossible.

—WALT DISNEY

Life is full of beauty. Notice it. Notice the bumblebee, the small child, and the smiling faces. Smell the rain, and feel the wind. Live your life to the fullest potential, and fight for your dreams.

—ASHLEY SMITH

To be healthy, wealthy, happy, and successful in any and all areas of your life you need to be aware that you need to think healthy, wealthy, happy, and successful thoughts twenty-four hours a day and cancel all negative, destructive, fearful, and unhappy thoughts. These two types of thought cannot coexist if you want to share in the abundance that surrounds us all.

—SIDNEY MADWED

The simple truth is that happy people don't generally get sick.

—BERNIE S. SIEGEL

Values-based happiness requires you to figure out what matters, then live a life that satisfies those desires and moves you in line with your values.

—POLLY CAMPBELL

When I look into the future, it's so bright it burns my eyes.

—OPRAH WINFREY

We turn not older with years but newer every day.

—EMILY DICKINSON

Wonder

Seeing the Beauty in Everything

IT IS OUR best tool to learning and understanding the world since birth. Just look at any baby's face and the wonder in those eyes looking out at the world, and you'll understand how mankind has become what it is today. Wonder moves us to understand and create things in our lives for the sake of betterment and most of all for the sake of happiness. I know wonder also led us into a lot of trouble as children, whether it was sticking a knife into a light socket or attempting to fly with one of our bed sheets from the roof to the garden. Nevertheless, wonder is the essential beginning for the journey to living successfully and with all the happiness you can find! You can't always be scared of something you don't understand; the only way to discover happiness is by embracing the wonder you see before you in this beautiful world and perusing the great experiences and teachings it offers to us, with joy and adventure in your heart.

Once we believe in ourselves, we can risk curiosity, wonder, spontaneous delight, or any experience that reveals the human spirit.

—E. E. CUMMINGS

There are no seven wonders of the world in the eyes of a child. There are seven million.

—WALT STREIGHTIFF

The soul should always stand ajar, ready to welcome the ecstatic experience.

—EMILY DICKINSON

Making the decision to have a child—it's wondrous. It is to decide forever to have your heart go walking around outside your body.

—ELIZABETH STONE

Think of all the beauty still left around you and be happy.

—ANNE FRANK

The fiercest agonies have shortest reign; and after dreams of horror comes again the welcome morning with its rays of peace.

—WILLIAM C. BRYANT

I feel no need for any other faith than my faith in the kindness of human beings. I am so absorbed in the wonder of earth and the life upon it that I cannot think of heaven and angels.

—PEARL S. BUCK

To see a world in a grain of sand and a heaven in a wildflower, hold infinity in the palm of your hand and eternity in an hour.

—WILLIAM BLAKE

Youth is happy because it has the capacity to see beauty. Anyone who keeps the ability to see beauty never grows old.

—FRANZ KAFKA

The world is full of magic things, patiently waiting for our senses to grow sharper.

—W. B. YEATS

Wonder is the beginning of wisdom.

—SOCRATES

We are an impossibility in an impossible universe.

—RAY BRADBURY

You'll never find a rainbow if you're looking down.

—CHARLIE CHAPLIN

Look at everything as though you were seeing it either for the first or last time. Then your time on earth will be filled with glory.

—BETTY SMITH

The invariable mark of wisdom is to see the miraculous in the common.

—RALPH WALDO EMERSON

Every moment of light and dark is a miracle.

—WALT WHITMAN

The more clearly we can focus our attention on the wonders and realities of the universe about us, the less taste we shall have for destruction.

—RACHEL CARSON

O, wonder! How many goodly creatures are there here! How beauteous mankind is! O brave new world, that has such people in't!

—WILLIAM SHAKESPEARE

wonder

I would rather have thirty minutes of wonderful than a lifetime of nothing special.

—JULIA ROBERTS

Because philosophy arises from awe, a philosopher is bound in his way to be a lover of myths and poetic fables. Poets and philosophers are alike in being big with wonder.

—ST. THOMAS AQUINAS

To live is so startling it leaves little time for anything else.

—EMILY DICKINSON

Wondrous is the strength of cheerfulness, and its power of endurance—the cheerful man will do more in the same time, will do it better, will preserve it longer, than the sad or sullen.

—THOMAS CARLYLE

Everything we put our attention on becomes more, bigger, and brighter.

—TONY BURROUGHS

The real talent worth having is the talent to be inquisitive and mindful, wondering about the world and taking every possible opportunity to create excitement and meaning.

—LISBETH CALANDRINO

wonder

Xanadu

Create Your Own Happy Place

MARCO POLO TRAVELED there and Samuel Taylor Cole-ridge scribbled out his most famous poem about the place, but besides being a summer capital for Kublai Khan in 12th-century China, Xanadu is a place that anyone can visit! It is the paradise that we all must find on our own, amongst the overcrowded streets and the never-ending bills; Xanadu is in the smiles of strangers and the blossoms of flowers. Experience life's pleasures and build your own sacred dome to keep your paradise in, so that whenever life goes awry, paradise is always a nearby place to escape to. Let it be the joy in your life when nothing else

seems to be going your way, the happiness
stored away in the face of everyday.

> *In Xanadu did Kubla Khan*
> *A stately pleasure dome decree:*
> *Where Alph, the sacred river, ran*
> *Through caverns measureless to*
> *man*
> *Down to a sunless sea.*
> —SAMUEL TAYLOR COLERIDGE

He who aspires to paradise should learn to deal with people with kindness.

—ABU BAKR

Aim at heaven and you will get earth thrown in. Aim at earth and you get neither.

—C. S. LEWIS

A happy family is but an earlier heaven.

—GEORGE BERNARD SHAW

You have to go on and be crazy. Craziness is like heaven.

—JIMI HENDRIX

Heaven is under our feet as well as over our heads.

—HENRY DAVID THOREAU

Xanadu, your neon lights will shine for you, Xanadu. The love, the echoes of long ago you needed the world to know: they are in Xanadu.

—JEFF LYNNE

Everything was chocolate ice cream and kisses and wind.

—FRANCESCA LIA BLOCK

That's right, there's free beer in Irish paradise. Everyone's jealous.

—KEVIN HEARNE

It's better to have your head in the clouds, and know where you are...than breathe the clearer atmosphere below them, and think that you are in paradise.

—HENRY DAVID THOREAU

The love of wilderness is more than a hunger for what is always beyond reach; it is also an expression of loyalty to the earth, the earth which bore us and sustains us, the only paradise we shall ever know, the only paradise we ever need, if only we had the eyes to see.

—EDWARD ABBEY

Certainly paradise, whatever, wherever it be, contains flaws. (Paradisiacal flaws, if you like.) If it did not, it would be incapable of drawing the hearts of men or angels.

—HENRY MILLER

Paradise was always over there, a day's sail away. But it's a funny thing, escapism. You can go far and wide and you can keep moving on and on through places and years, but you never escape your own life. I, finally, knew where my life belonged. Home.

—J. MAARTEN TROOST

By having good memories on every place you just visit, you are building paradise in your own heart and your life.

—TOBA BETA

A book of verses underneath the bough, a jug of wine, a loaf of bread—and thou beside me singing in the wilderness—and wilderness is paradise now.

—OMAR KHAYYÁM

Happiness is a garden walled with glass: there's no way in or out. In paradise there are no stories, because there are no journeys. It's loss and regret and misery and yearning that drive the story forward, along its twisted road.

—MARGARET ATWOOD

xanadu

Life is a paradise for those who love many things with a passion.

—LEO BUSCAGLIA

That's the difference between me and the rest of the world! Happiness isn't good enough for me! I demand euphoria!

—BILL WATTERSON

But when the sun in all his state illumed the eastern skies, she passed through glory's morning gate and walked in paradise.

—JAMES ALDRICH

The loves that meet in paradise shall cast out fear, and paradise hath room for you and me and all.

—CHRISTINA G. ROSSETTI

From the euphoric twinges of a new romance to the comforting reassurances of fingers entwined and hearts connected, our longing for love is universal.

—JUDY FORD

My idea of heaven is a great big baked potato and someone to share it with.

—OPRAH WINFREY

Connecting with your personal experience of heaven on earth opens the door to transforming your relationship in all aspects of your life.... The most potent way of connecting, renewing, and nourishing your experience of heaven on earth is through meditation.

—SUSYN REEVE AND JOAN BREINER

Don't wreck a sublime chocolate experience by feeling guilty. Chocolate isn't like premarital sex. It will not make you pregnant. And it always feels good.

—LORA BRODY

Poetry ennobles the heart and eyes, and unveils the meaning of all things upon which the heart and eyes dwell. It discovers the secret rays of the universe, and restores us to forgotten paradise.

—DAME EDITH SITWELL

Yes!

Grab On with Both Hands and Just Go for It

LIFE IS TOO precious to say no to your dreams and your happiness, so say *yes* instead! Remember that good intentions get you nowhere heavenly, so don't just think about doing it, put on your sneakers and "Just do it." Say yes to that someone who's asked you on a date, yes to the outfit in the window you've been dying to try on, but most importantly, say yes to your heart. Saying yes instead of no is the most positive and easy change you can make in your life. It is the magic word that opens the doors of opportunity and exciting new experiences. The ancient Romans never even had a proper word for *yes* and yet that never stopped them from taking action. So use the advantage that the English language gives us and say yes to start changing your life into a life of action and adventure!

Practice meditation regularly. Meditation leads to eternal bliss. Therefore meditate, meditate.

—SWAMI SIVANANDA

Choose a job you love, and you will never have to work a day in your life.

—CONFUCIUS

Dedicate yourself to the good you deserve and desire for yourself. Give yourself peace of mind. You deserve to be happy. You deserve delight.

—HANNAH ARENDT

Energy is an eternal delight, and he who desires, but acts not, breeds pestilence.

—WILLIAM BLAKE

Don't wait around for other people to be happy for you. Any happiness you get you've got to make yourself.

—STEWART EMERY

The time to be happy is now. The place to be happy is here.

—ROBERT G. INGERSOLL

y

If you want to be happy, set yourself a goal that commands your thoughts, liberates your energy and inspires your hopes. Happiness is within you. It comes from doing some certain thing into which you can put all your thoughts and energy. If you want to be happy, get enthusiastic about something.

—DALE CARNEGIE

Your success and happiness lie in you. Resolve to keep happy, and your joy and you shall form an invisible host against difficulties.

—HELEN KELLER

I have found that most people are about as happy as they make up their minds to be.

—ABRAHAM LINCOLN

The best way to secure future happiness is to be as happy as is rightfully possible today.

—CHARLES ELIOT

Our thoughts and imaginations are the only real limits to our possibilities.

—ORISON SWETT MARDEN

Everyone has inside him a piece of good news. The good news is that you don't know how great you can be! How much you can love! What you can accomplish! And what your potential is!

—ANNE FRANK

When a friend is in trouble, don't annoy him by asking if there is anything you can do. Think up something appropriate and do it.

—EDGAR WATSON HOWE

Trust no future, howe'er pleasant! Let the dead past bury its dead! Act—act in the living present! Heart within and God o'erhead.

—HENRY WADSWORTH LONGFELLOW

Nothing great was ever achieved without enthusiasm.

—RALPH WALDO EMERSON

Time wasted is existence; used is life.

—EDWARD YOUNG

Health is the vital principle of bliss, and exercise, of health.

—JAMES THOMSON

Do you want to know who you are? Don't ask. Act! Action will delineate and define you.

—THOMAS JEFFERSON

Do stuff. Be clenched, curious. Not waiting for inspiration's shove or society's kiss on your forehead. Pay attention. It's all about paying attention. Attention is vitality. It connects you with others. It makes you eager. Stay eager.

—SUSAN SONTAG

Life gives us choices. You either grab on with both hands and just go for it, or you sit on the sidelines.

—CHRISTINE FEECHAN

If you do things well, do them better. Be daring, be first, be different, be just.

—ANITA RODDICK

Doing the best at this moment puts you in the best place for the next moment.

—OPRAH WINFREY

Put on an outfit that makes you feel wonderful. It doesn't have to be over the top or designer-fab. It just has to make you feel great. Then go and get out of the house for a couple of hours.

—CAROLE BRODY FLEET

Love the moment. Flowers grow out of dark moments. Therefore, each moment is vital. It affects the whole. Life is a succession of such moments and to live each is to succeed.

—CORITA KENT

Shrug off the no's—they are temporary. This is your world. In your world there is only yes.

—JOLENE STOCKMAN

Zest

Change Your Future
by Changing Your Attitude

DON'T JUST ADD it to your food, add it to your life as well! Make sure you keep enjoying every day and never let life get dull. Put it in a cocktail or flare up your fashion sense with it, but always remember to add zest to your life because it is what makes each day more exciting than the last. Pursuing a zestful life will often entice creativity, passion and most importantly happiness to follow in pursuit. Say yes to zest! Nothing keeps you more alive than variety! It is what keeps life interesting, and what keeps *you* more interesting. So don't just slip into routine, zest things up!

Z

If you have zest and enthusiasm you attract zest and enthusiasm. Life does give back in kind.

—NORMAN VINCENT PEALE

True happiness comes from the joy of deeds well done, the zest of creating things new.

—ANTOINE DE SAINT-EXUPÉRY

Zest is the secret of all beauty. There is no beauty that is attractive without zest.

—CHRISTIAN DIOR

Passion is energy. Feel the power that comes from focusing on what excites you.

—OPRAH WINFREY

If things don't come easy, there is no premium on effort. There should be joy in the chase, zest in the pursuit.

—BRANCH RICKEY

In bad times and good, I have never lost my sense of zest for life.

—WALT DISNEY

To fulfill a dream, to be allowed to sweat over lonely labor, to be given a chance to create, is the meat and potatoes of life. The memory is gravy.

—BETTE DAVIS

Remember that happiness is a way of travel, not a destination.

—ROY GOODMAN

Our happiness depends on the habit of mind we cultivate. So practice happy thinking everyday. Cultivate the merry heart, develop the happiness habit, and life will become a continual feast.

—NORMAN VINCENT PEALE

Play keeps us vital and alive. It gives us an enthusiasm for life that is irreplaceable. Without it, life just doesn't taste good.

—LUCIA CAPACCHIONE

Each of us has a spark of life inside us, and our highest endeavor ought to be to set off that spark in one another.

—KENNY AUSUBEL

Variety's the very spice of life, that gives it all its flavour.

—WILLIAM COWPER

And 'tis my faith that every flower enjoys the air it breathes.

—WILLIAM WORDSWORTH

The greatest discovery of all time is that a person can change his future by merely changing his attitude.

—OPRAH WINFREY

But that's the whole aim of civilization: to make everything a source of enjoyment.

—LEO TOLSTOY

Boredom is the price one pays for not enjoying everything.

—MARTY RUBIN

The excitement of change and new beginnings can bring families together and give them a new life to look forward to. Simply look at the benefits and let them happen. No need to focus on the negative.

—DAVID MEZZAPELLE

[Walking] is the perfect way of moving if you want to see into the life of things. It is the one way of freedom. If you go to a place on anything but your own feet you are taken there too fast, and miss a thousand delicate joys that were waiting for you by the wayside.

—ELIZABETH VON ARNIM

zest

There are two ways to live: you can live as if nothing is a miracle; you can live as if everything is a miracle.

—ALBERT EINSTEIN

Though it may feel otherwise, enjoying life is no more dangerous than apprehending it with continuous anxiety and gloom.

—ALAIN DE BOTTON

Happiness is something you need to search for. It comes from inside. You can pull it out from inside by satisfaction and acceptance.

—VIJAY DHAMELIYA

It is in the compelling zest of high adventure and of victory, and in creative action, that man finds his supreme joys.

—ANTOINE DE SAINT-EXUPÉRY

I am a woman in process. I'm just trying like everybody else. I try to take every conflict, every experience, and learn from it. Life is never dull.

—OPRAH WINFREY

Life is more fun if you play games.

—ROALD DAHL

I never regret anything. Because every little detail of your life is what made you into who you are in the end.

—DREW BARRYMORE

Afterword
Make Someone Happy

THE HAPPINESS ALPHABET in this book is really a set of tools that allows for various approaches to self-growth and the inner work of self-development. These suggestions and inspired ideas vary widely, ranging from the more spiritual to the simple and practical.

I very much like the idea of undertaking inner work for self-development and working your way to a "better you." But I am also a strong advocate for believing in yourself and loving yourself each and every day. These are habits that can easily be reinforced in simple ways—journaling, writing affirmations, talking to yourself in the positive. I can see how some might think I have gone through my life like a horse with blinders, listening to the Joan of Arc-like voices in my head: "You are doing great!" Or some may assume that my life is wholly unexamined—certainly good arguments to be made. Yes, I do affirm myself and ascribe to some "woo-woo" notions about the power of the positive, but my point is this—it works. Self-belief is a simple and renewable source of what some call the state of *santosh,* or contentment. Like an engine that can drive you toward greater things, self-belief brings you closer to your purpose and your passion. Try it, give it some practice, and, above all, believe!

As a parting gift, I want to share with you what is now my number one way to feel better. It is something I learned from none other than Jimmy Durante, that gravelly-voiced singer of the good old days. His suggestion is to simply give someone *else* as much joy as you can, ensuring your own in the process:

It's so important to
Make someone happy,
Make just one someone happy...
Fame, if you win it,
Comes and goes in a minute.
Where's the real stuff in life to
cling to?
Love is the answer!

Make someone happy.
Make just one someone happy.
And you will be happy too.

About the Author

LOUISE BAXTER HARMON is a writer, gardener and eco-activist who lives in the San Francsisco Bay Area. Born in Gallipolis, Ohio, she learned the horticultural arts from her Aunt Ruth, from whom she also inherited her green thumb. Harmon also conducts writing workshops about "Putting Your Passion on Paper." Currently studying permaculture, Harmon is starting a seed-saving collective and working on a book on the healing power of gardening.

Index

to our readers

Viva Editions publishes books that inform, enlighten, and entertain. We do our best to bring you, the reader, quality books that celebrate life, inspire the mind, revive the spirit, and enhance lives all around. Our authors are practical visionaries: people who offer deep wisdom in a hopeful and helpful manner. Viva was launched with an attitude of growth and we want to spread our joy and offer our support and advice where we can to help you live the Viva way: vivaciously!

We're grateful for all our readers and want to keep bringing you books for inspired living. We invite you to write to us with your comments and suggestions, and what you'd like to see more of. You can also sign up for our online newsletter to learn about new titles, author events, and special offers.

Viva Editions
2246 Sixth St.
Berkeley, CA 94710
www.vivaeditions.com
(800) 780-2279
Follow us on Twitter @vivaeditions
Friend/fan us on Facebook